Capitalism's Toxic Assumptions

Capitalism's Toxic Assumptions

Redefining Next Generation Economics

Eve Poole

B L O O M S B U R Y
LONDON • NEW DELHI • NEW YORK • SYDNEY

First published in United Kingdom in 2015

Bloomsbury Publishing Plc
50 Bedford Square
London
WC1B 3DP
www.bloomsbury.com
London, New York, Delhi and Sydney

A CIP record for this book is available from the British Library.

ISBN: 9-781-4729-167-92

Design by Fiona Pike, Pike Design, Winchester
Typeset by RefineCatch Ltd, Bungay, Suffolk, UK
Printed and bound in India

For Katharine Isobel and Harriet Grace

Contents

Acknowledgements

A number of people read early drafts of the book or suggested examples or sources. I am extremely grateful to them for their help. They are, in alphabetical order: Marcus Alexander, Huw Bevan, Paul Bickley, Tim Binding, Michael Black, Simon Caulkin, Paul Davies, Matt Gitsham, Iain McGilchrist, Elizabeth Oldfield, Nathan Percival, Ed Poole, Thomas Poole, Patricia Riddell, Hamish Scott, Euan Semple, Nick Spencer, Stefan Stern, Richard Sweet and Brian Worsfold.

Foreword

When I was little, there was a stall at the local fair called Whac-A-Mole. To win, you had to hammer as many moles as you could, as they popped up randomly through a series of holes. In the arcade on Southwold pier, you can still play this game, but with bankers instead of moles. Banker-bashing is a lot easier than addressing the mess we've got ourselves into. It might be fun, but it's distracting. It masks a deeper problem, that the market as a whole is run by rules that are well past their sell-by date.

No one believes that the earth is flat any more, as early scientists did. Economists, on the other hand, haven't budged from their original world view. To make the system feel safe, the rules of the market are still described as fundamental laws of nature, which don't change over time. But even scientific truth is not this fixed, and economics has become a victim of its attempt to look credible. It's so stuck in the past that it's struggling to keep up with the facts as we see them today.

Market capitalism depends on seven big ideas. These have served the world well in the past, but over the years they have become cancerous, and are slowly killing the system as a whole. This means that the efforts currently being made to fix the aftermath of the credit crunch globally are a waste of time.

My sister was once stung by a bee. Luckily, we were staying at my grandparents, who were both medics. Grandpa fetched his stethoscope, and Granny got out her first aid kit, and in no time at all, my sister had an impressively bandaged foot. But she was still crying. Astonished by her ingratitude, they asked her what was wrong. 'It was the other foot,' she said.

With the markets, moving the odd deckchair won't stop the whole system crashing into an iceberg. We have to go back to the beginning and start again, or we'll just solve the wrong problem.

Your five-year-old has just been given a crisp £20 note from his Granny. He wants to know who the guy with the funny nose is. 'That's Adam Smith,' you say with confidence, 'the father of capitalism.' You realize your mistake when he says, 'What's capitalism?' 'Well . . .', you continue, slightly less confidently.

Have you ever sold anything on eBay? eBay is a great way to explain the market because it's such a pure version of the system. I want to pay for a holiday, so I sell off an heirloom. Strangers compete with each other to buy it, checking out the going price by looking at similar transactions. We don't know each other, but eBay's feedback mechanism acts as a guarantee, because no one wants to deal with someone dodgy, so everyone tries hard to keep their ratings up. The system means that I get my holiday cash, and the winner gets my heirloom. We're each acting selfishly in our own interests, but somehow everyone doing just that seems to work out over the longer term. If items don't appear on eBay very often, they spark off a bidding war and attract high prices. If they're everyday items, they tend to follow a predictable pattern, with prices staying fairly stable over time. Let's look more formally at the seven big ideas that sit behind this kind of market, as described by the guy on the £20 note, all those years ago.

First, the whole system assumes competition, on the grounds that it makes people try harder. This improves the quality of the market over time, as organizations vie with each other for market share, and people compete for jobs. Apple stays in the game by designing better products than its rivals. Supermarkets advertise price drops. And ambitious executives get an MBA to give them an edge in the job market. This is competition at work, improving the marketplace.

This welter of competitive activity is co-ordinated at the top by the so-called 'invisible hand'.This works imperceptibly, bringing together billions of customers and producers worldwide and matching supply to demand in such a way that everything works out right overall. What should be a chaotic mess somehow resolves into happy customers and rising profits, to the benefit of society as a whole.

And Adam Smith's biggest idea of all is that all we need to do to keep this process working is to be selfish: 'It is not from the benevolence of the butcher, the brewer, or the baker that we expect our dinner, but from their regard to their own self-interest.' Maximizing our own self-interest – or 'utility' – in any transaction we make leaves the 'invisible hand' free to do its work. While we look out for ourselves, it resolves everything for us in the system as a whole.

The way the 'invisible hand' does this is through pricing. The price of something acts as a signal to help match people who want to buy things with the people who want to sell them. Low prices attract more customers, while high prices restrict demand to a smaller circle. So everyday items like toothpaste are cheap and readily available, while products that are rare, like Old Masters, carry a high price. Changes in price affect buying behaviour, by making items more or less attractive. Provided governments let them be, markets use the ebb and flow of pricing to regulate supply and demand.

Within the system, people form organizations to generate wealth by producing goods and services. Most of these are companies, owned by the shareholders who provided the money to set them up in the first place. These owners employ people as their agents, to work for them. But, because the market works best when we all pursue our own ends, there is a danger that the interests of the owners and their employees will diverge, as each seeks to maximize their own utility. This conflict of interest is called 'agency theory', and means that a lot of HR policy is about incentivising employees to work in the interests of the owners.

Because the interests of the shareholders are so important, corporate strategy is always about how best to maximize shareholder value. This means keeping the share price high. Organizations use this barometer to set targets for staff; many grant their senior employees shares to make sure that the company's share price is always close to their heart.

And most of these companies are set up using the legal concept of 'limited liability'. This means that if the company folds, the owners will lose only the money they originally invested in it. This shields the owners from any downside, and so encourages people to invest. This flow of new capital is the lifeblood of the market, and is vital to keep the wheels of the market perpetually turning.

So far, so good. But if you zoom in on any of these firm foundations, they start to blur and wobble.

First, competition, the linchpin of the entire system. In fact, mathematicians would argue in favour of co-operation as a primary strategy, because it yields better outcomes over time. While winning at all costs is necessary for survival in war, in business, companies want longer term customer and supplier relationships. Those who treat transactions as battles to be won or lost sooner or later come a cropper, as their brand tarnishes and the market votes them out. On the other hand, co-operation and the sharing of information increases the size of the pie, instead of restricting the debate to arguments about how best to cut it up. And absolute competition isn't just mathematically questionable, it's sexist, too. While male fight-or-flight physiology favours competition, particularly in challenging environments, it ignores the role that female physiology has to play. Research conducted on female subjects suggests quite a different physiological response, one that has been dubbed 'tend-and-befriend'. So being hooked on competition may actually be compounding a tendency towards sub-optimal outcomes, reinforced through the norms of a traditionally masculine business environment.

Second, the 'invisible hand' is just an optimistic myth. It offers a reassuring but inaccurate justification for self-interested behaviour. While order does frequently rise out of chaos, there is no evidence to suggest that this always tends towards the good, and certainly none sufficient to justify society's reliance on it. The crowd is sometimes wise, but not invariably so. In fact, leaving things to the 'invisible hand' skews the market in favour of the strongest. This maximizes their utility, but not that of society or the world at large.

Third, the idea that 'utility' is the best way to measure the effectiveness and morality of the market works only if the 'invisible hand' really exists. This is because the concept is an empty one - utility for what? If there is no guarantee that individually selfish behaviours produce a good outcome overall, a system based on this thinking cannot be moral without help. And the sort of help this requires - government intervention - is exactly what the economists are trying to avoid, because it interferes with the smooth functioning of the market, and gets political, fast. Even if this idea was a sound one, the idea that 'Economic Man' is a rational agent is wildly optimistic. We are all subject to irrational urges, whether through peer pressure, emotions, or our psychological make-up. Assuming we are all robots just leads to confusion about how the market actually works, and about how best to run it.

Fourth, Adam Smith's original notion about the different interests of owners and managers has had catastrophic consequences. It has used negative psychology to generate HR policies that assume employee recalcitrance, limiting the ability of organizations to unlock human potential. Worse, it's been used to justify the disastrous ubiquity of executive shareholding. This practice, hand-in-hand with the idea of the supremacy of the shareholder, has made corporate strategy defiantly short-termist and manipulative.

Fifth, the assumption that the price mechanism, left to its own devices, will settle at a scientific equilibrium, is nonsense. It ignores the interplay between supply and demand, and the potential for both of these to be manipulated. As well as air-brushing out the historical debate about 'just' prices, market pricing ignores historical questions about cost. This obscures a very important debate about hidden costs (or 'externalities'), like the social cost of drinking or smoking or the cost of pollution. In an age where the limits of the Earth are starting to be felt, it is vital that this debate about the market's embeddedness is not ignored. There is now no cod left in Newfoundland, and the planet is running out of other commodities all the time.

Sixth, the belief in the shareholder as king owes more to a romanticized ideal about the nature of shareholding than it does to reality. Ignoring the extremely limited sense in which shareholders actually 'own' businesses, modern patterns of shareholding make the 'shareholder' a rather bizarre - and certainly fleeting - concept. The average time for which a share is now held? About 11 seconds. Blink and you'll miss it. Sticking to the romance that the shareholder is a nice old bloke who founded the company just drives short-termism. In an attempt to keep him in socks by keeping the share price high, companies neglect wider issues of accountability by ignoring other company stakeholders. This romanticism has fuelled the exponential rise of boardroom pay, and an overly narrow measurement of corporate performance. Many would now argue that shareholder value is the WMD of capitalism.

Seventh, the dominance of the limited liability model is extremely risky. In a global economy, the resilience of the system will always depend on diversity, so no one single model should prevail. In institutionalizing moral hazard, it also plays into an increasingly irresponsible shareholder culture, because there is no downside. More encouragement in law and public policy of alternative models for enterprise would introduce healthy 'competition' between business models. And more employee ownership and mutualization would spread risk, as well as creating a wider range of businesses with different risk profiles and models of success.

These core assumptions - capitalism's seven deadly sins - have got to be destroyed before a healthier system can be created, like a phoenix from their ashes. This book will examine each of them in more detail. First, where did they come from, and how have things changed since?

Introduction

Widely hailed as the patron saint of capitalism, Adam Smith wrote his *Inquiry into the Nature and Causes of the Wealth of Nations* in the decade between 1766 and 1776. By the time it was finished, he'd lived in both Scotland and England, and travelled widely on the continent, witnessing at first hand a range of economic models and arrangements. He was immersed in the intellectual milieu of the Enlightenment, and had strong connections with many prominent thinkers of the day, both at home and abroad. His *Wealth of Nations* has since assumed a life of its own. While few may have read it in its entirety, many regard it as the Bible of modern capitalism. But his famous book emerged from a particular context, and that context has now changed.

Picture Edinburgh in the 1770s. Population: 57,000. England and Scotland had formally united in 1707, so Edinburgh was governed from London by 'mad' King George III. Construction of the New Town had started, with North Bridge, Princes Street, Queen Street and the Mound having just been completed. Smith's friend, the philosopher David Hume, was living in the south-west corner of the new St Andrew Square, where the building that was to become the new headquarters of the Royal Bank was under construction. The Old Pretender, Bonnie Prince Charlie's dad, had just ended his life in exile in Rome, and the feud between the 'Jacobite' Bank of Scotland and its new competitor the Royal Bank of Scotland had been newly patched up, after the collapse of the Ayr Bank in 1772 required them to work together to restore stability.

During the 1770s, the Penny Post began, and stagecoaches were now going daily to Glasgow as well as to Newcastle and London – a journey that took two weeks. The Edinburgh-based

Encyclopaedia Britannica had just been published for the first time. Raeburn's famous 'skating minister', Rev. Robert Walker, was newly installed at Cramond. By this time, he'd probably already auditioned for the world's first skating club, which involved skating a complete circle on each foot, and jumping over a pile of three hats. In the west of Scotland, Robert Burns was writing his poetry, James Watt was perfecting his invention of the steam engine, and slavery was being challenged in the courts. On finance, Adam Smith was corresponding with Jeremy Bentham in London about interest rates, Edmund Burke was lobbying the government to repeal the tea duty levied on America, and the *Gentleman's Magazine* of 15 July 1773 recorded a resolution passed by the 'brokers and others' at New Jonathan's Coffee House in the City to rename it The Stock Exchange. Also in London, in 1775, the Thames' first Regatta delighted 200,000 spectators, while Richard Sheridan's plays were opening in theatres to critical acclaim. America declared independence in 1776, and the first bishop of the American Episcopal Church was consecrated soon afterwards by the Scottish bishops in Aberdeen. And in France, Louis XVI was grappling with the war-induced financial crisis that was to be the start of France's own revolution a few years later.

Adam Smith was baptised on 5 June 1723 in Kirkcaldy, which lies opposite Edinburgh across the Firth of Forth. His father had died five months before he was born. At the age of fourteen, he went to Glasgow College, where he was taught moral philosophy by Professor Francis Hutcheson, one of the first to lecture in English rather than Latin. In 1740 Smith won a scholarship to Balliol College, Oxford, where he spent the next six years. He then returned to Scotland, where he delivered public lectures in Edinburgh, and became close friends with

David Hume and Adam Ferguson. He became Professor of Logic at Glasgow University in 1751, transferring to the chair in Moral Philosophy when it became vacant the following year. His first book, *The Theory of Moral Sentiments*, was published in 1759. He remained in Glasgow until he was forty, when he resigned to take up a post as tutor to the third duke of Buccleuch, travelling with him on the continent, and writing what was to become *The Wealth of Nations* while he did so. The three-year tour gave him the opportunity to meet thinkers such as Voltaire and Quesnay before he returned with his charge to London in 1766. There, his employer had become Chancellor of the Exchequer, which gave Smith access to those wielding power just at the time when the American colonies were starting to rebel against the taxes levied on them to pay for the Seven Years' War. After spending six years writing in Kirkcaldy, he returned to London in 1773 where he finished writing *An Inquiry into the Nature and Causes of the Wealth of Nations* – published in 1776 – and was admitted to the fellowship of the Royal Society. Back in Scotland, Smith was made Commissioner of Customs in Edinburgh in 1778. Smith was elected Rector of Glasgow University nine years later, and died in Edinburgh on 17 July 1790, of a rather unromantic 'chronic obstruction' of the bowel. He was buried in the Canongate churchyard in a tomb designed by Robert Adam, his kinsman from Kirkcaldy. Just before his death, he ordered the destruction of sixteen volumes of manuscripts, which has focused subsequent attention on his three key works, *The Theory of Moral Sentiments, The Wealth of Nations*, and the posthumously published *Essays on Philosophical Subjects* (1795).

Since Adam Smith's day, the marketplace has changed dramatically. Edinburgh's population has increased tenfold to 500,000. Scotland has returned to a form of self-rule, with a devolved parliament, and the terms of the union between Scotland and England are under review. The journey from Edinburgh to London now takes about four hours, travelling via the modern descendent of Watt's steam engine, or under an hour by aeroplane. The equivalent of the Penny Post remains, but is under threat from the ubiquity of electronic messaging. The internet has transformed the business landscape. The UK leads the world, with an internet economy that *The Economist* reports already constituted over 8 per cent of GDP by 2010, and which is now bigger than its construction and education sectors. This digital revolution has also defeated Smith's venerable contemporary, *Encyclopaedia Britannica.* Famously approached by Microsoft and offered an early chance to participate in the CD-ROM market, which morphed into *Encarta, Encyclopaedia Britannica* rather grandly dismissed the overture on the grounds that 'we are in the book business', and has now largely disappeared. Rescued from bankruptcy in 1996, in 2012 they announced their retreat from books, and finally accepted a deal from Microsoft for a digital tie-up with its search engine, Bing.

In Smith's day, manufacturing was just starting to become the dominant industry, as was richly depicted in his books. Now, 81 per cent of the workforce work in the services industry. Big business in general has reached proportions that might have amazed him, in spite of the international reach and power of some of the companies of his day like the East India Company and the Dutch East India Company. For example, in the UK alone, Tesco has a supermarket in every single postcode area the length and breadth of the land, and the turnover of modern multinational companies is often quantified in comparison with the GDP of nation states. While companies are not countries, and turnover and GDP are not really comparable measurements, the juxtaposition makes for eye-catching results. In *Business Insider*'s 2011 comparison, Walmart is bigger than Norway, Chevron is bigger than the Czech Republic, General Electric is bigger than New Zealand, Amazon is bigger than Kenya, and Nike is bigger than Paraguay.

Modern banking is now a very different industry. According to Bank of England data, while the UK in the mid-nineteenth century had around 500 banks and 700 building societies, between 1825 and 1913 the number of banks in England and Wales fell from over 600 to around seventy. At the start of the twentieth century, the assets of the UK's three largest banks together accounted for 7 per cent of GDP. A century later, their assets stood at 75 per cent and, by 2007, had risen to 200 per cent of GDP. Looking more widely at the sector as a whole, UK banking assets now stand at over 500 per cent of GDP, a ratio exceeded only in Iceland, Luxembourg and Switzerland. Like the Ayr Bank, modern banks still collapse, as Lehman Brothers did in 2008, but their scale means that many of them are now deemed 'too big to fail'. While the Bank and the Royal Bank are still major Edinburgh institutions, they both suffered during the 2008 credit crunch and had to be rescued from collapse by the government. The Royal Bank Group became 84 per cent owned by the UK government, which, having brokered the rescue of the Bank of Scotland by means of a Lloyds Banking Group takeover, also owns 41 per cent of the resulting organization.

That old coffee house, the London Stock Exchange, is now the fourth largest stock exchange in the world. Modern trading has increased exponentially in scale, speed and complexity. Looking just at trading in equities, in 1885 around sixty domestic manufacturers and distributors were listed on the Stock Exchange. By 1907, there were almost 600, and by 1939 that number had almost tripled to 1,712. As of 2012, there were 2,938 companies from over 60 countries listed on the London Stock Exchange, with an average daily trading volume of around 612,000 trades. On the New York Stock Exchange, 962 million shares were traded in 1962, as compared with 262 *billion* in the year 2000. Nowadays, $2 trillion changes hands every day on the foreign exchange markets alone, and $7 trillion on the global stock markets.

Modern dependence on electronic transactions for financial deals has also introduced an interesting dimension to the political use of economic sanctions. In Smith's day, ports could be blocked or protectionist taxes levied (the Boston Tea Party famously epitomizing both a protest against an unwelcome tea duty and a subsequent harbour blockade) but when the EU decided to apply economic sanctions to Iran, all they needed to do was switch off the SWIFT codes that are used to send payments to Iranian banks. This prevented those banks from transferring funds to and from other worldwide banks, effectively turning Iranian international commerce into a barter operation.

While Adam Smith might be amazed by the modern market, in some ways capitalism has not really changed, as illustrated by the eBay example above. It still enables the generation of surplus wealth by joining together in markets the owners of capital, the organizations that use it, and the customers who consume the products and services these organizations generate. The resulting market uses the mechanism of pricing to achieve equilibrium between supply and demand, with competition ratcheting up performance over time and preventing monopoly induced market failure. An 'invisible hand' works to combine individual self-optimization into collective utility, and the workings of the market are underpinned by the rule of law. The state's role is both to regulate and to prevent or correct market failures through government intervention.

As for any system in use, an account of capitalism and how it works requires a number of assumptions to be made for that account to hold true. While these are legion, there are some meta-assumptions that are so core to the DNA of modern capitalism that they are foundational to our understanding of the market. First, competition, widely assumed to be the hallmark of a healthy market, and fiercely protected through legislation in order to prevent monopoly and customer exploitation. Second, the 'invisible hand' that co-ordinates myriad individual market transactions into outcomes that benefit society as a whole. Third, utility as the key measure of economic benefit, whereby each person – in maximizing their own utility, given a competitive market where individuals act in their own self-interest – will generate an ethically sound outcome, courtesy of the aforementioned 'invisible hand'. Fourth, agency theory, which holds that the interests of the owners of capital and those employed as their stewards will naturally diverge, such that considerable cost and ingenuity is needed to create some alignment between them (given a rather gloomy view of the worker as shirker). Fifth, the assumption that market pricing settles at an equilibrium that is fair, given the match it implies between supply and demand. Sixth, the widespread acceptance of the supremacy of the shareholder, and the efforts made to enshrine this priority in corporate strategy. And seventh, the ubiquity of limited liability as the model of choice for enterprise, because it allows investors to provide financing while risking only their original stake, instead of taking on a wider set of potential liabilities which might otherwise scare them off. These assumptions were made at particular points in history when they were so obviously true they were assumed to apply universally and forever. But the passage of time has shown that many of these assumptions are now open to challenge. These faulty foundations or 'toxic assumptions' need to be updated before capitalism can safely evolve into a more resilient system. Only by reassessing the very foundations of capitalism can the entire system be strengthened.

This idea of 'toxic assumptions' is not peculiar to economics. What the jargon calls a 'paradigm shift' tends to be evidence that a toxic assumption has been overturned. Whether it is realizing that the earth is not flat, or the heliocentric universe of the Copernican Revolution, or the discovery of fossils and evolution, these shifts in understanding are almost as disorientating as the discovery of plate tectonics. Often these shifts demand a response that feels counter-intuitive, or one that literally turns known truth on its head, like banishing the earth from the centre of the universe, to be replaced by the sun. In medicine, vaccination is a good example of this topsy-turvy logic. In the late eighteenth century, it would not have seemed sensible to those who had taken the Hippocratic Oath to deliberately infect a healthy person, until they found that giving people the relatively benign disease cowpox prevented them from catching the contagious and deadly disease smallpox, because they developed an adaptive immunity to it.

There is a poignant exhibit in the Grant Museum of Zoology in London. It is an old jar of plastic dinosaurs. The label explains that these much-loved toys represent the history of our evolving understanding of dinosaurs. As more fossils have been discovered, more types have been identified. It turns out that the brontosaurus is a juvenile version of the previously discovered apatosaurus, for example, and triceratops has just been 'disambiguated', with the newly named torosaurus being introduced to explain differences in the famous horns and neck-frills. This exhibit is a perfect metaphor. In science, temporary hypotheses - or potentially toxic assumptions - have always been seen as the necessary roads to progress. A hypothesis generates a theory that is held until evidence emerges to disprove it. The modern scientist now scoffs at alchemy and phrenology, not to mention the idea that the humours could be rebalanced by blood-letting, but it was these assumptions that paved the way for later insights. Newtonian physics was challenged by Einstein, who in turn is being challenged by data emerging from CERN's Large Hadron Collider. Science ultimately welcomes each upheaval as a sign that mankind is moving closer towards the truth.

Not so, however, in the 'science' of economic theory, where old assumptions seem to have assumed the role of precious artefacts, to be protected and even venerated in perpetuity. My argument is that economics needs to be more scientific in this regard, and to rejoice in dispensing with old ideas in favour of better ones, rather than clinging on to them at any cost. At the same time, economics also needs to be rather less scientific, given its tradition of the rather robotic 'Economic Man' as a predictable ideal, and its image of the market as a machine that is susceptible to fine-tuning. Recognizing the reality of human agency and the complexity of markets as systems may not sit comfortably in a scientist's mind, but would lead to more realistic economic analysis and more accurate problem-solving.

Much of economic theory concerns capitalism, and it remains the prevailing orthodoxy. This book looks specifically at seven of the foundational assumptions of capitalism and where these have begun to threaten healthy progress in the future. These toxic assumptions need urgently to be tackled, and challenges to them used as levers to initiate reform of the system as a whole. The book examines each toxic assumption in turn, looking at why it has become unstable, and how it might be updated or repaired for the future. Where possible, we'll meet thinking and practices that are already detoxifying, and, where these are thin on the ground, discuss some ideas about where to start.

Chapter 1

The assumption of competition

Perhaps one of the most familiar quotes from *The Wealth of Nations* is this one: 'People of the same trade seldom meet together, even for merriment and diversion, but the conversation ends in a conspiracy against the public, or in some contrivance to raise prices.' For hundreds of years, this spectre has been used to reinforce the central idea of competition in market economics, without which we fear that the system would descend through price-fixing into monopoly, and the customer would suffer. Indeed, this core pillar of capitalism is the most compelling argument that economists have against Communist-style centrally planned economies, because they replace competition with centrally agreed prices and result in a stagnating market.

The idea of competition is fundamental to the way we think. At school we are encouraged to try to beat the other children in tests and at sports, and there is an annual revolt in the tabloid press when schools are too 'politically correct' to award prizes at sports days. We are encouraged to view other schools as rivals, and at home our parents are as worried about 'keeping up with the Joneses' as we are about having the latest cool gadget of the day in the playground. Whether through sports or music or clubs and hobbies, we learn early how to compete and are rewarded for winning. While losing is 'good for the character' we also learn that it is the price to be paid for trying, and we resolve either to quit, or to win next time round. After leaving school, we compete with others to win a place at college and then get a job, where we learn about 'competitors' and become skilled at second-guessing their strategies in order to outwit them. Even in fields where traditional competition is not evident, we compete in league tables or for funding. And every weekend there is sport to watch, the central drama of which is the competition.

Competition is taken not only to benefit the customer by driving down prices, but also to drive improvement in goods, services, processes and performance over time, so it is upheld by a complex array of law and regulation, all designed to keep the market healthy. However, on closer examination, this assumption of absolute competition between similar firms is flawed on at least two counts. The first is to do with maths, and the second is to do with gender. These will be examined in turn, before looking at a better way of understanding when competition is useful and when it is counter-productive.

First, the maths, and specifically game theory. Game theory, a method of studying strategic decision-making, is a branch of mathematics that looks at situations where the success of one party's choices depends on the choices made by another party. Mathematicians have reduced these situations of conflict and co-operation between rational decision-makers, which they call 'games', to their mathematical skeleton for the purposes of analysis and comparison, and their findings have been applied to politics, computing, psychology and biology, as well as to economics. An example of one famous type of 'game' is called the 'prisoner's dilemma'. This scenario involves two suspects being arrested and imprisoned by the police. Because the evidence is insufficient for a conviction, the authorities need at least one of the suspects to confess in order that both might be implicated. The prisoners are placed in separate cells, and the police visit each in turn to persuade them to confess. Obviously, if both prisoners remain silent, both will go free. If both confess, both will be sentenced. If only one confesses, they could negotiate a reduced sentence in return for their co-operation. Given that the prisoners have no way to communicate, they have to guess how the other will act, and respond accordingly. Simple scenarios like this one are used by game theorists to spot patterns and rules about how we interact with others, and can be used in a wide variety of settings. For example, the prisoner's dilemma is the basic 'game' behind the arms race, in many trade and treaty negotiations, and in any situation where co-operating or defecting are the basic choices available. Such 'games' can be modelled as one-off interactions, or can be iterated over time to see how strategies change in the light of past behaviour and experience.

Applying game theory to economics is not new, and game theory is not as esoteric as it used to be, since the Oscar-winning film *A Beautiful Mind* popularized it by telling the story of the famously schizophrenic game theorist John Nash. But game theory offers a serious challenge to received wisdom about competition. According to this received wisdom, the working assumption is that companies operating in the same markets are in conflict with one another, in a battle for market share. This is encouraged by the regulatory framework, because of the damage collusion can do to the interests of the customer. However, in gaming terms, the solution to a game will not materially alter if the parties co-operate rather than compete, and defection is only a superior strategy when the interaction is a singular event and the players will never see each other again. This flatly contradicts the usual argument that competition automatically produces better outcomes. Indeed, there is a positive value attached to the fact of co-operating. This is because a period of co-operation essentially reduces risk by allowing the parties to test beforehand a wider set of bargaining options than they might have had the chance to use in the actual game, as well as to learn about their opponent's gamesmanship, thereby increasing the amount of information available and enhancing the set of possible outcomes.

One of the scenes used in *A Beautiful Mind* serves to illustrate this concept. John Nash and a group of male friends are in a bar when a beautiful blonde enters, accompanied by a bevy of brunettes. Hollywood has Nash's mathematical brain analyzing the available outcomes, thereby formulating his Nobel Prize-winning Nash Equilibrium Theory, the original 'win-win' strategy. In the film, Nash realizes that in order for all of his friends to end up with a girl, the best strategy is for all of the guys to choose a brunette. That way, everyone gets a girl. If not, those who fail with the blonde are likely to be rejected by the brunettes for having regarded them as second best, so there is a high degree of risk that no one gets a girl. By playing this 'game' co-operatively, all players win. This 'strategic sub-optimization' (no one gets the blonde) in mathematical terms increases the range of possible outcomes, shifting the focus from a win/lose arrangement about sharing the 'pie' to one that tries to identify a larger pie, so that all parties emerge better off.

This simple idea, that increasing the amount of information available generates better outcomes, is particularly intriguing in the context of the market, where it is often by taking advantage of imperfect information that one party gains over the other. This is encapsulated in the so-called Grossman–Stiglitz paradox, which holds that if a market were informationally efficient, such that all relevant information was reflected in market prices, then no single agent would have sufficient incentive to acquire the information on which prices were based. This would mean that there would be no point in seeking advantage through superior market knowledge, i.e. taking positions and trading securities, and any sort of market that traded on asymmetries of information would essentially cease to exist. This is perhaps a *reductio ad absurdum*, but information as a commodity in and of itself is becoming increasingly important, both to companies and to states. Eric Schmidt, former CEO of Google, once estimated that the total of all human knowledge created from the dawn of man until 2003 would total five exabytes (10^{18}). A recent report by Cisco, however, suggests that by 2015, internet traffic will reach 966 exabytes, and the US National Security Agency is currently building a facility in Utah with the aim of storing a yottabyte (10^{24}) of global information, the equivalent of one million exabytes, or 500 quintillion pages of text. Such projects, and the increasing processing power of computers, brings a business strategy based on maximizing information within reach, particularly given the mathematical arguments in its favour. Incidentally, this would also remove one of the arguments against state control of assets, whereby central planning is seen to be less efficient than market pricing because of the information this generates about supply and demand.

There have been numerous books seeking to introduce thinking about co-operation and information-sharing into the mainstream. In 1984 the political scientist Robert Axelrod produced *The Evolution of Co-operation*, building on an earlier paper he had written at the University of Michigan with the evolutionary biologist William Hamilton. This book described a competition established by Axelrod to evaluate alternative strategies for playing the prisoner's dilemma 'game', expressed as 62 different computer programmes, to enable a grand tournament that could be iterated over time. The most successful strategy was also the simplest. The winning strategy, TIT FOR TAT, co-operated on the first move and mirrored the other player's moves thereafter. Axelrod developed this tournament into a mathematical model to show how co-operation based upon reciprocity emerges even in a population of egoists. His model showed that with only a small cluster of reciprocators, such a population can resist 'invasion' by mutant strategies. Further, the only time when defection is a superior strategy is when the interaction is a one-off and the players will never meet in future. His collaboration with William Hamilton to investigate precedents for this behaviour in evolutionary biology resulted in an article in *Science* in 1981, which won them the American Association for the Advancement of Science's Newcomb Cleveland Prize.

Axelrod's work led him to suggest four properties for successful strategic behaviour. First, players should avoid unnecessary conflict by co-operating for as long as their opponent does. Second, players should retaliate in the face of an uncalled-for defection by their opponent. Third, players should 'forgive' their opponent after responding to a defection. Fourth, the player should display clarity in their behaviour, so that their opponent can learn and respond to the strategy deployed. Because it is the prospect of meeting again that encourages the instinct to co-operate, Axelrod also suggests that clever strategists 'enlarge the shadow of the future'. In society this has traditionally been achieved by making transactions public through ceremonies, speeches or contracts. Other gambits involve the use of deals or tie-ins so that the person has an incentive to trade with you again in the future, or the breaking down of interactions into smaller transactions so that the parties can build familiarity, confidence and trust over time.

Axelrod has a caveat. Apart from a tendency for people to behave less altruistically if there appears to be no prospect of repeat business, in a zero-sum game (one where, by definition, one party wins at the expense of the other losing) it is in fact useful to keep the other player guessing, and therefore to be more covert than Axelrod would otherwise suggest. This is because the doubt such a move introduces renders your opponent less efficient, which can only be to your benefit. But Axelrod would argue that genuinely one-off zero-sum games are comparatively rare, particularly as far as reputations are concerned, and making the wrong diagnosis means that the outcome of any future meeting is jeopardized by bad behaviour at the outset. This is why your mother told you never to be rude to strangers, in case they turn up on a future interview panel. When this thinking is applied to markets, there are so few genuinely one-off transactions or relationships that assuming the kind of zero-sum model that underlies a need for absolute competition is simply an inaccurate rendering of the situation.

In 1996, Barry Nalebuff and Adam Brandenburger, at that time at Yale and Harvard respectively, wrote a book called *Co-opetition*. It extended this logic of strategic co-operation into business, which generally obliges parties to interact over time. Their title was designed to capture the dynamic interplay between co-operating (to create or expand the pie) and competing (to divide it up). Their aim was to assist businesses in applying game theory to corporate strategy, drawing particular attention to the role of 'complementors', or those parties who may also be competitors, suppliers or customers, but whose products and services enhance the value of your own when both are acquired together. This particular sort of collaboration is already enshrined in many joint ventures and partnership agreements, but game theory would argue for its extension into the adoption of a co-operative mode more generally, because the more information that is available, the better the set of available outcomes. To the traditional executive, this sounds very dangerous, and immediately conjures up images of Smith's warning about price-fixing meetings in dark rooms filled with cigar-smoke, a serious and potentially devastating claim to which we shall return.

But before we return to the danger of price-fixing, why, when the maths is widely accepted and has been popularized through a number of well-received books, is co-operation not a more central part of the DNA of business? The reason for this is my second objection to an unquestioning acceptance of competition as the only game in town, and is based on gender. The sociological observation that men are keen on sport has spawned endless caricatures. While this is endearing, it has a dark side. The police report a sharp increase in domestic violence when favourite teams lose key games. This phenomenon has everything to do with the reason that competition is still the default in market economics. Markets are invariably run by men, and men are biologically conditioned to respond to perceived threats by competing to win. While this was biologically necessary when we were prehistoric, it is only sometimes necessary in the modern world, and less necessary in the modern business context than could be assumed from its ubiquity as an axiom.

The biology is simple and widely understood. In dangerous situations, the body responds in 'fight-or-flight' mode, producing adrenaline to boost performance. Among other things, adrenaline raises the heart rate to increase blood flow, dilating the blood vessels and air passages to increase the likelihood of survival either through physically combatting the threat or fleeing from it. While this has often been explained as a binary choice, the body in fact defaults to 'fight' and resorts to 'flight' only if the person involved does not feel adequately resourced to prevail. Indeed, this is why the primary stress reaction is so alluring, because the 'fight' mode is characterized by a temporary enhancement of both physical and neuro-biological functioning to give us the best possible chance of surviving. It is only when it becomes apparent that all is lost that the body prepares for flight, and brain functioning reduces to focus on physical exit. Many performers both in sports and the arts rely on this enhancement, and the low brought on by the adrenal hangover is notorious. This idea that a certain amount of stress enhances performance has given rise to the terminology 'eustress' or good stress, as opposed to 'distress' or bad stress. This state also gets called the 'stretch zone', and current theory suggests that it can be extended by increasing the range of situations in which a person feels either physically or psychologically resourced to prevail. The downside of being in an aroused state is that the body thinks it is straining to survive, and under pressure we may perceive threats to survival that actually do not exist. As the body moves into flight mode, cognitive functioning shuts down, and we overestimate our abilities to overcome a threat just when our ability to make this judgement becomes seriously impaired.

What is less well understood is that this response is not a universal one. It is a male one. Before 1995, only 17 per cent of test subjects in this field were women, and the 'fight-or-flight' theory was originally based on studies on male rats. When these studies were carried out on humans, results from female subjects were discounted because variations in hormone levels caused by female reproductive cycles meant that their data was often confusing or difficult to interpret. But Shelley E. Taylor and her colleagues at the University of California became curious about why the data from females didn't fit, and wondered if it was the theory that was at fault, rather than the test subjects. When the tests were rerun, it became apparent that the 'fight-or-flight' theory was predicated on the existence of testosterone. When women were involved, the stress response triggered the release of oxytocin instead, the 'love hormone' associated with peer bonding, affiliation and motherhood. Their paper, published in the *Psychological Review* in 2000, contrasted the male 'fight-or-flight' response with the female response which they dubbed 'tend-and-befriend'.

Maybe in a male-dominated world it is not surprising that the paper has received scant attention (except in the women's magazine *Marie Claire*), and that funding to pursue these experiments has been slow to materialize. Its findings suggest that men are conditioned to react to stressful situations by reading them as zero-sum games and meeting them head-on as a matter of life and death. This is usually explained as a difference in role from our cave-dwelling days, when the men were responsible for hunting and defence and the women for tending the fires and the children. In these conditions, 'fight-or-flight' would give cavemen an evolutionary edge. Similarly, a stress response in women that was more about 'tend-and-befriend' would enhance their ability to carry out their role under pressure. A protective response towards offspring, and the seeking out of social contact for mutual support and protection, would help to keep the fires and the children safe while the men scared off the sabre-toothed tigers. Today, this response is pilloried in adverts about women gossiping on the phone, which only shows how intuitively we have understood this difference all along, even if we have not always understood its social function.

Of course, we are not prisoners of our biology, and many women who have spent their careers working alongside stressed men may find that over time they have developed a Pavlovian 'fight-or-flight' response, and can no longer remember experiencing 'tend-and-befriend' instead. But it is interesting to wonder whether, given free rein, a 'tend-and-befriend' response in the boardroom would not be more useful than a 'fight-or-flight' one, given theories about the usefulness of co-operation. As an example, the particular trigger for the recent credit crunch was banks refusing to lend to each other. We have since learned that this was made all the more complex because the banks were manipulating the LIBOR inter-bank lending rate anyway. The resulting impasse locked the system, triggering the liquidity crisis that toppled so many institutions. Given statistics on gender balance in the boardroom, most of the senior people involved in the situation were men, likely trying to make good decisions in enormously pressured conditions. And it is highly probable that the long working hours they were putting in over that period, and the effect this had on the quality of their sleep, let alone the impact of the crisis on diet and exercise, would have primed their body chemistry for 'fight-or-flight' no matter how rational they thought they were being about it. It would have involved quite staggering amounts of self-control to override such strong biological instincts to protect their own bank at all costs, in what must have seemed a very extreme zero-sum game environment, particularly when formal economic theory about competition would provide them with a rational defence for self-interested action. Perhaps a group of women would have acted in the same way. But suppose 'tend-and-befriend' had kicked in instead. The instinct to pick up the phone to discuss it with the others might just have offered the banking community an opportunity to share information and to work together to keep the system functioning, given that a collapse in confidence in banking affects the system as a whole.

This hypothesis would be supported by the work of Cambridge's John Coates, himself an ex-trader, whose research shows the magnifying effects of testosterone and cortisol on male trader behaviour, and that, under stress, the weighting of probabilities becomes more distorted among men relative to women. This argues for the involvement of more women, as well as older people whose testosterone levels have diminished, in order to smooth the risk profile of trading, particularly under stress. More generally, the 2011 Davies Report on women on boards included the finding that companies with more women on their boards significantly outperform their rivals, with a 42 per cent higher return in sales, 66 per cent higher return on invested capital and 53 per cent higher return on equity. The 2010 data from McKinsey on top-quartile companies also shows that the return on investment (ROI) of those with the highest proportion of females on their executive committees exceeds by 41 per cent the ROI of those with wholly male executive committees. Similarly, the operating results of those with mixed-gender boards exceed their male counterparts by 56 per cent. Additionally, the economist Mikko Manner has shown that having a female chief executive is positively correlated with superior corporate social performance, and a recent study for a UK asset management firm, reported in *New Model Adviser* in 2011, found that FTSE-listed companies with at least 20 per cent female representation at board-level achieved significantly higher operational and share price performance, both in the short and the medium term, than those with lower percentages of female representation. One caveat: research always shows that heterogeneous groups make better decisions than homogeneous ones, and it may be that women are merely used in these studies as a cypher for 'diversity', given how unrepresentative so many boards still are. But the argument from stress research would suggest that women have a specific role to play in difficult times, in keeping lines of communication open when the instinct might otherwise be to shut them down. And if we are to believe what maths tells us about more information generating better outcomes, this could only improve corporate results.

But how best to achieve co-operation in a way that benefits the customer, the organization and shareholder, without falling foul of accusations of 'price-fixing'? Perhaps the idea of 'comparative advantage' rather than Michael Porter's more popular 'competitive advantage', provides a clue. David Ricardo's 1817 explanation of comparative advantage used examples of wine and cloth in England and Portugal, but the notion can be put more simply. Apparently, Winston Churchill was a gifted bricklayer. But he was also a gifted politician and author. When he needed a wall built, he chose to pay builders to do his bricklaying for him, even though he could have done the work better himself, so that he could spend his time on the activity where he had relative - or comparative - advantage. Linked to the ideas of division of labour, specialization and opportunity cost, comparative advantage is the invitation to focus your effort where you can best generate a tradable excess. In some sense, comparative advantage is about generating intrinsic competition, to hone whatever talent it is that you have, like 'adaptation' in evolutionary biology. While this is with a view to trading the excess for a margin, it is different from competing externally, where you may never attain absolute advantage. Although it is activity carried out in the light of there being a market for the talent you are developing, the agenda is set by the talent, rather than the activity of other players in the market. Trying to outpace competitors, on the other hand, locks you into an agenda set by them. If they downsize, outsource or cut prices, the logic of competitive advantage suggests that you should do likewise. The logic of comparative advantage argues instead that you should focus on the area of activity where you are at your best.

As London Business School's Gary Hamel has explained in his critique of Michael Porter, a 'me too' strategy based on absolute competition inevitably leads to 'corporate liposuction' as competitors match each other's incremental changes in a race to the bottom. Hamel favours the rule-makers over the rule-takers, because they find the as-yet un-colonized 'white spaces', following Wayne Gretzky Sr's advice to 'skate to where the puck's going, not where it's been'. Price wars among the supermarkets are a case in point. Those who compete 'enough' but keep a focus on their comparative advantage will tend to emerge as stronger brands over the long term, like the Waitrose and Marks and Spencer food offers in the UK. Their competitors, differentiating on price, become commodities in comparison. And a commodity strategy attracts little customer loyalty, especially with the dawn of internet shopping, making each weekly shop a zero-sum game rather than part of an ongoing and profitable co-operative relationship.

As well as playing to comparative advantage, there is still something to be said for harnessing the dynamics of competition, when it can improve performance. In the sixteenth century, Machiavelli recommended the invention of an enemy if there was not one conveniently to hand, in order to keep the people fit and united. In the eighteenth century, Adam Smith argued that good management could only be universally established within a competitive environment, because this would force everybody to have recourse to it for the sake of self-defence. But learning the lesson from game theory that *planning* to play the game is as much of a game as playing the game itself, perhaps the correct posture for business in the twenty-first century is to optimize performance by playing co-operatively *as if* to win. However, this does require a sophisticated mental attitude in the minds of everyone involved. Companies need to recognize that they cannot ultimately win at the expense of their competition and that co-operation yields better economic outcomes, while still acting competitively enough to maintain fitness in the marketplace, and to respond to the needs of their customers and the regulator. An analogy would be the difference between war and sport. Winning still matters a great deal in both, but in war, the traditional aim is to obliterate your opponent. In sport, players often train together, and while one may win, it is in their interest to nurture the opposition, lest their removal from the game prevent future opportunities to compete.

Another analogy from sport is that of the role of pacesetter. If you do not have your competition there to egg you on, will you be able to stay the course on your own? As most companies have found, the existence of a competitor helps to keep focus, to aid innovation, and to encourage the longevity of a company. This does indeed benefit the consumer, but if this attitude could be upheld while companies also collaborated, albeit under the watchful eye of the regulator, the benefits to shareholders would be increased too. Of course, there should properly be a limit on this co-operation, not least to satisfy the regulator and avoid price-fixing. Indeed, to ensure that co-operation does not become cartel, the regulator should play the role of 'stooge' on the customer's behalf in order to ensure a residual level of competition between the parties. In the game theory sense, the stooge's role is to stimulate competition by offering parties attractive coalition deals. In a regulatory sense, the relevant authority achieves this by setting guidelines and boundaries, for example on price or market-share. In any case, it is important to understand the underlying rules of the game before deciding which to break. But the message from the game theorists remains that in an environment where reputation and relationship is important, co-operation yields better outcomes than competition.

And Axelrod holds that this is best guaranteed by 'enlarging the shadow of the future' to provide the necessary incentive for co-operation. He says this is most successfully achieved by a combination of making the transaction durable, making the interactions frequent, and by breaking the transaction down into small steps so that both parties can learn to trust each other in stages. For example, a public commitment to a partnership, or an announcement that is reported in the media, makes both parties loath to look like they have changed their minds because of the reputational damage this might attract. This has long been a political negotiation ploy, to tie one's hands with an 'announceable' so that a position looks unassailable, but here it can be used more positively to signal and confirm intent. And making transactions frequent makes the next loom larger so that it acts as an immediate reminder of the need to co-operate. Many organizations use this manoeuvre to keep customers loyal, by offering vouchers or deals that expire within the next month to attract a rapid repeat purchase, or by offering loyalty cards to lock customers in and competitors out. Indeed, one way to understand brand as a concept is to see it as an attempt to convert a 'transaction' into a 'relationship' to avoid customer defection. Organizations seeking to co-operate with each other could do this by agreeing upfront a programme of joint projects, with meeting dates prearranged at suitably close intervals, or by arranging informal or social meetings in the gaps between them. This process could also assist with Axelrod's recommendation to co-train each other up gradually, by agreeing in the first instance small pilots or experiments to test compatibility before embarking on major collaborations. Some organizations who are thinking about pooling their back-office operations have sometimes started the process by sharing basic recruitment or payroll services and building up from there, and a number of formal mergers or joint ventures have begun in this way.

In case this seems naïve, given the overwhelming cultural resistance to it, some examples might help to explain why this could improve outcomes. Apart from routine co-operation over industry standards and codes of practice (the rules of the 'game'), broadly, there are three main types of co-operation within the 'game' itself. The first type is common and tends not to attract much attention. This type is co-operation within the supply chain, over design, marketing, etc., including Nalebuff and Brandenburger's 'co-opetition' with complementors. This type ranges from conversations between supermarkets and their suppliers over packaging and display, which would include those suppliers who make supermarket-branded goods to be sold alongside their own, to collaboration between Intel, IBM and Microsoft in delivering personal computers. It might also include more unusual collaborations, such as the use by NGOs and government agencies of the Coca-Cola delivery network in Africa to distribute medical supplies. The second type is more overt co-operation between traditional competitors, but it is usually sanctioned through formal joint venture agreements or heralded as a prelude to a merger. Examples would be the Orange and T-Mobile announcement that their customers could now use both networks – followed by similar announcements from Vodafone, with O2 and Three – or when airlines swap loyalty schemes or code-share flights. However, it is properly the third type of co-operation that has the most potential, but which is fraught with regulatory traps. Some of this co-operation between direct competitors is informal, like the common use by taxi firms or hotels of their rivals to cope with overflow or spikes in demand, particularly for key customers. Some is organized by the state, like OPEC, or the Belgian brick cartel set up in the 1980s to allow a failing industry time and space to recover. And some is episodic and project-based, when consortia are formed to take on large infrastructure or finance projects, like the building of a new bridge, or the rescue of a distressed organization by a group of private equity funds, for which no one player has sufficient scale. And sometimes competitors sign up for common systems to gain scale in areas that are not deemed core, like the Interflora network or Frontline, the distribution company set up by magazine publishers, or the member-based Cheque and Credit Clearing Company in the UK.

Co-operation to create new markets, to build scale or to share expertise, for the right reasons, allows companies to focus on those areas where they can genuinely add particular value. In launching the CD market in Latin America, the music industry agreed that, since there was not enough volume to make it worthwhile for them all to have their own plants, one of them would produce the product for them all, leaving each free to focus on branding and distribution. So companies like Virgin never needed to invest in physical production, but could achieve the lowest manufacturing costs in the industry by partnering with the cheapest provider. In Scotland, the Glen Ord distillery carries out malting for a large number of competing malt whiskies for the same reason, and many aggregate companies collaborate in optimising loads to keep delivery costs down.

Research and development is another area where co-operation is often found, as long as the relevant regulator is convinced that the benefits of it outweigh any resulting weakening of competition. For example, in the automotive industry, it is common for competitors to share knowledge and expertise regarding fundamental pieces of design work that would be hard to amortize over their own expected volumes. The chassis and basic shell components of the Volkswagen Sharan, the

Renault Espace and the Peugeot MPV are largely the same, allowing each brand to differentiate over other design factors. Similarly in aerospace, given the complexity involved, the development of the Tornado military jet was a joint consortium between BAE Systems and their equivalents in Italy and Germany, and the Airbus consortium is just the latest in a series of alliances created to develop individual aircraft over the years.

These kinds of co-operation help to reduce the duplication and inefficiency which is the downside of competition. If two - or more - firms compete absolutely, they have to duplicate much of their activity. While this usefully creates jobs, it also wastes resource, whereas sharing efforts would release resource to be used productively elsewhere. Where firms are clear about where precisely they have advantage, they can pool their resources, both to benefit from economies of scale, and to free them up to focus more exactly on where they can genuinely add value.

However, a key challenge in the area of co-operation between competitors is the balance between healthy co-operation, designed to serve the customer and society, and cartel-style collusion. The dark side of game theory proving that working together can optimize outcomes is that it can also be used to provide the business case for cartels if customers are left out of the 'game', hence the role of the regulator to act as their proxy. But regulation tends to be a fairly blunt instrument, and Adam Smith's original warning about price-fixing looms so large that in reality few competitors want to risk trying anything in that vein. Two contrasting examples illustrate this point. First, the universally popular collaboration between the banks and the credit card companies to launch 'Chip and PIN', the new common standard for the authorization of credit and debit cards to reduce fraud across the industry. The regulator applauded this initiative. Similarly, the recent agreement between Coca-Cola and PepsiCo to switch the type of caramel used to colour their colas in order to avoid Californian regulation about warning labels for suspect carcinogens, has been widely perceived as a customer-focused move. There was a different result, however, when Unilever and Procter & Gamble worked together with other competitors through a trade association to try to migrate customers to detergents that could work equally well in lower volumes. Given Unilever's track record in corporate social responsibility, this was unlikely to be just about profits, given their work in parallel on cold-water detergents. Yet in 2011 the regulator fined both parties £280m for price-fixing, because the introduction of new packaging required the parties to agree to march in step until the transition had been completed. Perhaps these examples are too simplistic, but they serve to illustrate the thin line between what appears to be 'good' co-operation and what appears to be 'bad'. The washing powder example in particular shows why so many companies are loath to implement green initiatives, given that they risk market share in doing so, but cannot be seen to be discussing the issue with their competitors.

Because of the ingrained opposition to competitor collaboration, this is one of the assumptions whose toxicity will take the greatest effort to unravel. More empirical research is needed on gender differences, coupled with positive discrimination to correct imbalances in board representation. Wholesale review of regulation is also required, to check where it still serves the customer and the economy as a whole, and where it merely shores up an unhelpful orthodoxy that sub-optimizes market outcomes. As an example of how challenging this will be, the UK's 1998 Competition Act states rather baldly: 'Agreements between undertakings, decisions by associations of undertakings or concerted practices which may affect trade within the United Kingdom, and have as their object or effect the prevention, restriction or distortion of competition within the United Kingdom, are prohibited.' While this is hedged about with exceptions, its core message is clear, and to unpick it - and parallel arrangements in other countries - will be a mammoth task. Apart from regulatory changes, companies themselves will need to make careful adjustments to find the right path between healthy co-operation and unhealthy collusion without falling foul of the regulator. As the London-based economist Paul Ormerod has shown, regulation that serves purely to intensify competition eventually reaches a point where it starts acting against the health of the system rather than promoting it, because co-operation is also crucial for the system's health, and getting this balance right will not be easy.

Meanwhile, many companies use overtly legitimate vehicles to drive co-operative activity, the most common of which is the outsourcing of non-core activity to third parties, or the use of independent consultancies to produce 'benchmarking' data or to devise new operating systems and processes. Many organizations are also affiliated to the relevant trade or professional association both for personnel and commercial reasons. This use of sanctioned intermediaries is well-established. It facilitates the legitimized sharing of competitor information and in the case of outsourcing can represent a useful cost-management exercise in its own right. In any procurement process, it's often a provider's experience of working with competitors that attracts new custom, as organizations know they will then benefit from 'recycled' industry data. These kinds of activities could be used both more strategically and more proactively, but it would be too easy a solution to outsource as much as possible and just keep close the one area of business that is distinctive. What might be more fruitful is for the corporate strategists to meet with the relevant regulator to map out those areas where collaboration would be in the interests of the customer and the industry as a whole, and to confirm those areas which need to be reserved in those same interests. Similarly, as companies meet, they would need to be more transparent about the mode that they were in. Software companies like SAP both compete and collaborate with consultancies like Deloitte and providers like Oracle, and so need to signal their agenda in each interaction to avoid accusations of 'anti-competitive' practices. Interestingly, the UK government's recent review of competition arrangements offers an insight into what companies might do to reap the benefits of co-operation without falling foul of existing regulation. In re-examining the criminal cartel offence, the government has decided to redefine the offence to replace the 'dishonesty' test with a 'secrecy' test. Cartel behaviour – price-fixing, agreements to limit supply or production, non-compete agreements or bid-rigging – is still an offence under competition law, with a fine of up to 10 per cent of turnover. However, it is no longer a criminal offence if the parties involved have agreed to publish details of those arrangements in the *London Gazette* (one of the official journals of record of the British government) before they are implemented, so that their customers are aware of them. This is a technical change, designed to increase convictions. But it suggests that if companies are not engaging in cartel behaviour when they talk to their competitors, all they need to do to avoid trouble is to make their discussions public, or at least invite the regulator along.

In the Judaeo-Christian tradition, there is a story about Naaman, the commander of the armies of Syria. He has leprosy, and his boss the king hears that there is a prophet in Israel who might be able to cure him. Laden with gold and silver, Naaman sets out, and arrives with his horses and chariots at the house of Elisha. Rather than coming out to greet the great man, Elisha sends him a messenger, telling him that if he goes and washes in the Jordan seven times, he will be cured. But Naaman, expecting drama, is so angry that that he is being fobbed off with something so prosaic that he leaves. Eventually, he is persuaded to give the Jordan a go, and is cured. I think the toxic assumption of competition is like this story. It could be fixed with a huge drama involving massive legal and cultural change. Or it could be cured very simply. If companies simply publicize any conversations they have with their competitors – whether privately with the regulator or publicly to their customers – and promote more women, over time the balance between competition and co-operation will adjust. But, as Naaman found, this does require a massive leap of faith.

Chapter 2

The assumption of the 'invisible hand'

One of Adam Smith's most famous legacies is the idea of the 'invisible hand' that supposedly leads the individual actions of all players in markets to work out in the best interests of society as a whole. The term first appears in Smith's early essay on the 'History of Astronomy', published posthumously in 1795. This usage refers to the 'invisible hand of Jupiter' in a discussion about the use of God or Gods to explain irregular events in nature. He refers to these types of explanation as important sociologically because they 'soothe the imagination' when people are perplexed by the mysterious, so perhaps it is unsurprising that he then appropriates the term for his own use in explaining the 'magic' of the market.

In the context of economics, the term appears in his *Theory of Moral Sentiments* (1759):

> The rich are . . . led by an invisible hand to make nearly the same distribution of the necessities of life, which would have been made, had the earth been divided into equal portions among all its inhabitants, and thus without intending it, without knowing it, advance the interests of society.

The term appears again in *The Wealth of Nations* (1776):

> He generally, indeed, neither intends to promote the public interest, nor knows how much he is promoting it . . . he intends only his own gain, and he is in this, as in many other

> cases, led by an invisible hand to promote an end which was no part of his intention.

In Smith's world, where religious belief was the norm, the idea of some kind of external benevolence or divine plan made so much sense that few thought to challenge this claim, and it has persisted as an assumption ever since. But why would it be logical for individually selfish actions to somehow cancel out into general benefit? It does seem true that supply and demand tend to meet at a point of equilibrium, but it need not follow that the sum total of all of these matches creates public good. As David Jenkins, the famously outspoken former Bishop of Durham, puts it:

> In a cool and detached hour how could anyone possibly imagine that a global system whose basic dynamic was competitive self-interest could, of its own momentum, promote the prosperity and freedom of all?

Indeed, we know that the market over time adjusts to mirror the desires of those creating it through the sum total of their actions. And as anti-capitalist commentators like Tim Gorringe have argued, policies that favour a free market automatically favour the rich, since the market responds to those who have the most ability to participate, and thus the only way the net outcome could be benevolent is if the desires of the rich and powerful were themselves benevolent.

Exposing the 'myth' of the 'invisible hand' became the life's work of Michigan State University's Warren Samuels, who died just before the publication of his magnum opus on the subject in 2011. He dedicated years of his life to tracking down and analyzing references to the 'invisible hand', amassing several thousand books, ten filing cabinets and several large boxes of notes on the subject. His magisterial analysis leads him to conclude that the notion of the 'invisible hand' has in fact been rather cynically used, in Smith's own terminology, to 'soothe the imagination', and as 'psychic balm' to facilitate social control. He explains that its ephemerality as a concept allows those in power to use it as a talisman to justify their attempts to gain control. Markets use it to argue that they should be left alone; governments use it to justify 'corrective' interventions; and the term in general is bandied around to reassure the populace that everything will somehow magically just come right if only we leave it to those in charge. Many other writers in social theory and other disciplines have discussed similar use of mythical devices as tools of social control, whether it is Marx on religion as the opium of the people, or our parents on the tooth fairy and Santa Claus. The theologian Graham Shaw has also written about the careful use of religion to displace responsibility all the way up through the hierarchy until it is passed off to God, who conveniently cannot be produced 'in the dock' to give an account of himself.

The moral philosopher Mary Midgley would be particularly worried by the use of the word 'hand' in this context. She argues that personification, while rhetorically attractive, actually contributes towards the powerlessness that this kind of displacement creates. In her book on *Wickedness*, she points out that:

> A melodramatic tendency to personify physical forces and other scientific entities can represent them as demons driving us, rather than humble general facts about the world, which is all they have a right to be seen as. This produces fatalism, which certainly is incompatible with a belief in free will, since it teaches that we are helpless in the hands of these

> superhuman beings ... Writers whose point is really just to show us some general fact about the world are led on with astonishing ease, by way of saying that we cannot change this general fact, to treating it as if it were itself an agent manipulating human beings, and as if all real human agency had been absorbed into it.

Apart from the general usage of 'the invisible hand' as a convenient and controlling fiction, Samuels identifies four ways in which the term has tended to be used in practice. Primarily, it is used to explain the auto-efficiency of a competitive market. Second, it has also been used by the economist Friedrich Hayek to explain unintended or unforeseen consequences and spontaneous order. Third, it is used to explain the result of the interaction or aggregation of market transactions and, fourth, as a positive term to suggest that markets only ever produce benevolent outcomes. The Nobel laureate Joseph Stiglitz has argued that 'Smith's hand was not in fact invisible: it wasn't there'. Before agreeing with him, we need to examine all four of these usages in turn.

We can dispense with three of these usages in short order. Taking the last first, it is logically incoherent to suggest that the sum total of diverse transactions must 'by definition' be benevolent, given the lack of data to support this claim. Such an assertion makes sense only if it is based on faith. Since economics prides itself on being a science, to uphold a belief in a benevolent 'invisible hand' would be bizarre. Next, its usage to explain the result of the interaction or aggregation of market transactions. In some sense the term can function as a useful shorthand in this instance, given how impossible it would be to describe the sum total of market interactions and transactions. But it isn't so much an 'invisible hand' as millions of different hands whose collective efforts produce 'the market' day by day. So whether this usage adds anything is a moot point, unless it is functioning as 'psychic balm' again, to reassure us all that someone somewhere has an overall picture of all of this complexity. This is of course illusory, and formally impossible without positing the existence of a deity, another worry for many a scientist. This same argument also finds wanting the use of the 'invisible hand' to explain the auto-efficiency of a competitive market. The idea of a free market is to facilitate the matching of supply and demand. Efficiency is theoretically achieved when supply and demand achieve equilibrium and the market clears. Again, 'the invisible hand' is a useful rhetorical device to suggest that there is some logic to this process, but it goes too far to suggest that a hand 'leads' the matching process in this way, given that no one player in the marketplace could occupy such a position of Archimedian privilege. That markets tend towards efficiency is in any case largely unproven, given that no 'pure' market exists to provide the necessary evidence.

The remaining use, as offered by Hayek, needs more attention. As we have seen, Hayek uses the concept of the 'invisible hand' to explain unintended or unforeseen consequences and spontaneous order. In this, he was influenced by Adam Smith's friend, Adam Ferguson (1723–1816), who described the phenomenon of spontaneous order in society as the 'result of human action, but not the execution of any human design'. In looking for a way to explain why order spontaneously emerges, and why actions often have unintended or unforeseen consequences, Hayek used the motif of the 'invisible hand'. Again, its function is largely rhetorical and to reassure, but the idea of there being something 'designed' about spontaneous order has recently come back into vogue. One example that would seem to support the idea of an 'invisible hand' is 'swarm intelligence', which takes its inspiration from the natural world. Ant colonies, bird flocking, fish schooling and animal herding are all examples of systems where those involved follow very simple rules, and, in the absence of a central control structure, the local and often random interactions between them lead to 'intelligent' group behaviour, as when flocks of starlings or shoals of fish spontaneously change direction. This could be used as an analogy for market behaviour, if following the simple rule of self-interest generated 'intelligence' at the level of the market as a whole. But here another example is instructive. Squirrels are notorious for burying nuts in the autumn so that they have something to eat in winter. This suggests that they have a sense of the future, and the ability to plan ahead. But studies show that this is not the case. In fact, they just see other squirrels hiding nuts and copy them, and in general this means there are enough nuts hidden that a given squirrel will find about as many as they themselves have hidden, although they seem only to stumble across their own by accident. It is thought that migration might also operate in this way. So there are already two types of crowd behaviour, one of which appears to add up to collective wisdom, another of which seems to do so accidentally and inefficiently. A third type of crowd behaviour has been dubbed 'the wisdom of the crowd' and is the same as the theory behind the price mechanism and much statistical thinking. This idea is that taking into account the collective opinion of a group of individuals – asking the audience – is better than seeking the opinion of a single expert. Thinking of the classic bellcurve, the 'noise' of bias, subjectivity and error created by an isolated data point is smoothed out through the averaging process to reveal a consensus view. But in all three cases any 'invisible hand' in play is not necessarily benevolent. The fish could school right into the mouth of a shark, the squirrels could fail to find the nuts they need, and the crowd could universally agree on an erroneous course of action. As we will see in the discussion of pricing, the 'wisdom of the crowd' in the market for human kidneys may establish a settled price (it costs on average $150,000 to buy one; you get $5,000 if you sell yours) but this does not make the price - or the trade - 'right'.

However, it is clear that the seemingly random actions of self-interested individuals can appear somehow ordered, or can at least result in surprising coherency, making the 'invisible hand' seem plausible. Indeed, an element of the flagship strategy course at Ashridge Business School used to involve an exercise in the beauty of randomness. Over dinner, participants would take it in turns to roll two dice, calling out the number as they did so. Each number corresponded to a note on the scale, and the dice rolls were used to compose a piece of music. After dinner, the piece was played on the cello, in the darkness of the chapel, and always seemed eerily beautiful. But, as we have seen, there is nothing to suggest that this coherency has to be by definition harmonious or benevolent. This point repays some examination. As we will see later on, self-organizing self-interest can result in overfishing as readily as it can create from nowhere a sizeable market for Fairtrade coffee. And while there is a suggestion from game theory that good will out, it is unclear to what extent this theory can describe the total working of the global market in perpetuity. This is because while evolution favours co-operative strategies, these require agents to adopt them consciously - or at least visibly - and, as noted above, to be influenced by the likelihood of future meetings to continue to behave well. The reality of the modern market makes creating this necessary 'shadow of the future' simultaneously much harder and much easier. Most transactions are now carried out largely anonymously with strangers and through intermediaries, destroying a key incentive for co-operation. This is immediately remedied where technology facilitates feedback, like the ratings that buyers leave for sellers on Amazon and on eBay, such that the threat of reputational damage within a given trading community acts as a proxy for a repeat transaction with the same person. If two items are priced the same and are in the same condition but one seller has a higher feedback rating, I will be more likely to trust that person with my money than their less popular competitor. This system is increasingly used for products and on consumer websites for tradespeople, restaurants and other service providers. But such proxies are still no guarantee. Were there to be what the economist Donald Hay calls perfect 'reputational mechanisms' in the market, there would be no need for external moral constraints, because everyone would have to behave well in order to be able to keep participating. This was one reason that the Quakers achieved competitive advantage in business, because their reputation for honesty and self-regulation made them less risky and therefore ultimately cheaper as business partners. However, until there is total transparency, this remains an ideal, and a person is still better off, mathematically speaking, if they act selfishly in a one-off transaction.

Apart from a first order concern about terminology, a look at the actual workings of the market reveals that the deck is loaded against 'fair' or benevolent market outcomes, because only those able to participate in the market can influence it, and those with the most power within the market can influence it the most. Paul Ormerod is particularly known for his use of sophisticated modelling techniques to see how markets really work. Starting with the prosaic observation that the behaviour of an individual can be directly affected by the behaviour of others, he builds up a view of the market which is at odds with the orthodox view, in which economists have had to assume that the tastes and preferences of individuals are fixed for their models to work. Partly, he admits, this is because traditional machine-oriented maths was not able to cope with situations in which behaviours change because of the behaviour of others. Systems in which individuals copy each other need different techniques of mathematical analysis, and these have become available only in the last few decades, as has the required computer modelling power.

Because 'the market' is created by individual actions and interactions that influence others in the market, it is what is now referred to as an ever-changing 'complex adaptive system'. In order to determine whether this tends towards benevolence or is neutral or negative, we have to try to dig underneath all these layers of complexity to determine where the centre of gravity really is, and where the bias of the market falls. A key characteristic of complex adaptive systems is their susceptibility to nudges, because they are such delicately balanced ecosystems. Those market players that provide the most nudges are thus most likely to be able to influence the market in their favour. In the world today, it is generally the richer nations that have this power, as do the rich and powerful within these countries. As a trivial example, today in the UK many market towns have lost their fishmonger but gained a fish spa, where the well-heeled can have a Turkish pedicure carried out by *Garra rufa* fish. They have to drive to an out-of-town supermarket to buy the fish for their supper, though.

However, it is at the macro level that we can more clearly see the huge bias in the global marketplace towards the richer nations. While this is slowly changing, IMF data on global trade flows between 1960 and 2005 show that the countries of the northern hemisphere remain the dominant destination of global trade. Traditionally, this has been because the south depends on northern capital goods, finance, technology and export markets, and can only reciprocate with the production and export of a narrow range of primary commodities. The growth of economies such as India and China is already shifting this pattern overall, and stimulating intra-southern trade flows like the market for India's cheap generic drugs or China's insatiable appetite for commodities. But the north continues to do better out of the globalization of the market than the south, and still seems to hold all the cards, with many developing countries locked in an uneven relationship with their northern neighbours regardless of respite initiatives like the Jubilee 2000 campaign to relieve them of some of their debt obligations. As the Marxist geographer David Harvey puts it, the capitalist class is profiting at the expense of the health of capitalism as a whole.

Apart from trade flows, the developed world also takes advantage of the developing world's cheaper and more lax operating conditions in order to keep prices down. This has led to much controversy, from Cadbury's use of indentured labour in West Africa at the start of the twentieth century, to Brooke Bond's starving tea-pickers in Sri Lanka in the middle of the century, and Nike's use of sweatshop labour in Indonesia at the close of the century. Currently, Apple is facing sharp criticism over suicide rates at one of its factories in China, and in 2013 the

Rana Plaza factory fire drew attention to the human cost of the supply chain choices of a range of high-profile brands, including Walmart, Primark, Matalan and Monsoon. Most companies can argue that as their overseas outsourced operations are not legally owned by them, they have no responsibility for working conditions. Luckily, consumers don't agree, and campaigns like 'Lift the Label' have forced the hands of many companies to act to protect the integrity of their brand. But there are still too-frequent exposés of companies across the industries who do not act responsibly abroad, the latest of which has been Glencore. Famously the largest ever stock market debut, Glencore floated in 2011, valued at $61 billion. The commodities company has recently been implicated in human rights abuses and pollution in several of its countries of operation, and many of its colleagues in the extractive industries have had similar charges levelled at them over the years.

Additionally, the historical bias in World Trade Organization membership allows the developed world to maintain protectionist practices that help their own industries at the expense of those in less powerful countries, who they insist must liberalize trade as a condition of IMF funding. For example, it has been estimated that each US farmer receives in subsidies roughly one hundred times the income of a corn farmer in the Philippines. Subsidies payable under the European Union's Common Agricultural Policy represent over 40 per cent of the entire EU budget, which in 2006 amounted to a payout of around €50 billion. Thankfully, the much-criticized textile equivalent, the Multi Fibre Arrangement (MFA), finally expired in 2005, but large textile tariffs and quotas remain in place to protect first-world industry. In Europe, the end of the MFA was marked by a tense diplomatic stand-off with China, as China moved early to avoid an impending reduction in its export quota. Dubbed the 'bra wars', 80 million items of Chinese-made clothing were intercepted and held in warehouses at European ports, including 11 million bras. This necessitated the intervention of Peter Mandelson, then EU trade commissioner, to broker a deal between Beijing and the EU's twenty-five member states to resolve the matter, handing a golden photo opportunity to the tabloid newspapers.

These protectionist tendencies allow the rich to manipulate the 'invisible hand', and have become increasingly complex and problematic as a result of the technological advantage that richer nations hold over poorer ones. Intellectual property rights, which include the protection of copyrights, trademarks, patents, industrial design rights and trade secrets, tend to protect the developed world disproportionately, and this has become particularly problematic in the realms of medicine and in the life sciences, where types of grain and even human genes have now been patented. Currently, intellectual property is protected internationally through the WTO's Agreement on Trade-Related Aspects of Intellectual Property Rights (TRIPS). As an indicator of magnitude, IMF data shows that the US made $105.6 billion from the export of intellectual property in 2010 through licensing fees and royalties (next on the list is Japan at $26.7 billion, followed by Germany at $14.4 billion and the UK at $13.8 billion). The developing world has complained that TRIPS is used in an overly narrow and mean-spirited way by the more advanced economies, particularly in relation to life-saving drugs. The pharmaceutical companies argue that they need to protect their patents in order to recover the investment made in the development of such products, without which there would be no incentive to develop them in the future. But this argument does not necessarily stack up, given that developing countries account for only 10 per cent of global drug sales. Africa's drug bill as a whole is only 1 per cent of total world spend. As an example of what has been dubbed 'biopiracy', hundreds of the indigenous plants used in traditional Indian medicine have now been patented by Western pharmaceutical companies and are therefore protected under TRIPS, including turmeric (used as an antibiotic), neem (also known as 'village pharmacy' for its cure-all properties and used variously as an anthelmintic, anti-fungal, anti-diabetic, antibacterial and antiviral treatment, as well as a contraceptive and sedative), and stonebreaker (used for jaundice and hepatitis). As we have seen, the zero-sum thinking that informs these moves is of course 'normal' in an environment where competition is paramount.

Whether it is the range, availability or price of products, the official market, the one that is regulated, has been shaped by the strong for the strong. The 'invisible hand' is delivering utility for them, but not for the rest of the world. So those for whom participation is hard or impossible, or for whom the market's products and services hold no appeal, have had to create their own markets. The Peruvian economist Hernando de Soto reckons that 'extralegal' sectors in the developing world account for 50–75 per cent of all working people, and are responsible for anywhere between a fifth to more than two-thirds of the total economic output of the Third World. In his book *Stealth of Nations*, Robert Neuwirth estimates the size of the 'informal economy' to be $10 trillion worldwide, making it the second-largest economy in the world after the United States. Indeed, rather than regarding these 'grey' markets as suspicious, the market proper has a lot to learn from them. Even the market in counterfeit goods may be more beneficial than has often been supposed. In 2010, an EU-funded report co-authored by the Durham criminologist David Wall showed that goods like fake handbags may indeed help luxury brands by generating brand loyalty among people who could yet become future customers, as well as stimulating demand for hyper-exclusive originals in a race to the top.

Likewise, careful observation of grey-market behaviour can generate useful opportunities for creating 'bottom of the pyramid' business models as a way of correcting the bias of the 'invisible hand'. Mobile telephony is one such example. There are now more mobile phones in Africa than there are in North America. Rather than copying the slow evolution of Western telephony, mobile technology offers the developing world a way to leapfrog ahead. For example, Motorola has developed a $40 no-frills mobile phone specifically for emerging markets; it has a battery life of 500 hours for villagers without regular electricity, and extra-loud volume settings for use in noisy markets. In Africa, companies such as Vodafone and Visa have devised ways to use mobile phones as platforms for banking and other transactions in order to address market access issues for the three-quarters of the world's poor that the World Bank estimates are un-banked, often living in shanty towns and rural areas. The 2012 data from On Device Research suggests that in Kenya, which has the highest penetration, 96 per cent of mobile phone users use their devices to conduct financial transactions, and this becomes a general average of 53 per cent when data is included from Ghana, Nigeria, India and Indonesia. Together, these technologies could transform scattered and impoverished communities into viable and thriving economies.

Charities, social enterprises and enlightened multinationals move ceaselessly to create new markets for the poor, establishing products that over time are likely to be absorbed into the market proper. ToughStuff and SELCO have pioneered the use of solar power and rechargeable batteries in Africa and India to fuel lights, mobile phones, radios and sewing machines. MIT's Amos Winter spent time in Tanzania and noticed that wheelchairs were designed with the developed-world user in mind. Without a health service that can lend out expensive equipment and enforce legislation about accessibility, the estimated 20 million people in emerging economies who need a wheelchair have to resort to hand-powered tricycles that are too large for indoor use and too heavy to move over rough terrain. So Winter designed a lever-powered mobility aid, like a mountain bike, that could cope with hills and mud as well as paved streets. Further, it was constructed with easy-to-source bicycle parts, so that it could be repaired easily and cheaply at a local bike shop. In India, in response to a need for clean and affordable cookers, BP developed a hybrid cooking appliance that integrates liquefied petroleum gas and a biomass burner to reduce indoor pollution. Their offer includes home delivery, an LPG cylinder and micro-financing for the initial capital cost. And in South Africa and India, HP has introduced a new solar-powered digital camera and backpack printer, distributed through self-help groups for local women. Villages can also rent a video projector, a DVD player and speakers. Cheap wireless computers are available too, with antennae made from recycled tin cans.

Many of the business models established by the charity sector, like micro-credit and fair trade, have now been mainstreamed by commercial operators, both in the developing world and closer to home. Parallel financial markets have also emerged, legally sanctioned or otherwise, with the widespread adoption of micro-finance and the use of local currencies. San Francisco's Kiva, a micro-finance organization that facilitates on-line peer lending to the developing world, has a 99 per cent repayment rate. Indeed, now that the charity sector has demonstrated the attractiveness of the micro-finance market through organizations like Oikocredit, Shared Interest, Opportunity International and Five Talents, banks are increasingly entering the sector for commercial gain. This, like the adoption of own-brand fair trade lines by the large supermarkets, is not unproblematic, and many worry that this mainstreaming may in time erode the impressive advances made in these areas. But both examples serve to show how the not-for-profit sector can blaze a trail for the rest of the market to follow, helping more people gain access and enabling the marketplace to respond to their needs too.

But participation requires finance. In a climate where banks are reluctant to lend and the interest rates in the payday loan market are prohibitive, first-world peer-to-peer lending platforms like Zopa and Funding Circle are now thriving. Credit unions, too, are flourishing, with the World Council of Credit Unions estimating activity in over 100 countries for 188 million members, with $1.5 trillion in assets. These range from countries like Barbados and Belize, where over 65 per cent of the economically active population belong to a credit union, to the US and Canada where around 45 per cent of the population are members. In Ireland, three-quarters of the economically active population belong to a credit union. Recent support in the UK by the Church of England should also see British take-up improve.

Alternative currencies, too, are emerging, the most famous of which is bitcoin, the peer-to-peer virtual currency whose market capitalization reached $10 billion at the end of 2013. But most alternative currencies are physical not digital, and their illiquidity facilitates their primary use as a support for the local economy. For example, Bristol has the 'Bristol Pound' to help keep money spent locally active within the city's economy, because research by the New Economics Foundation suggests that every pound spent with a local supplier is worth £1.76 to the neighbourhood economy as opposed to a mere 36p if it is spent in a chain store. In London, Brixton's banknotes are collectors' items in their own right, depicting local characters like David Bowie, as well as James Lovelock and van Gogh. The UK has around 300 such Local Exchange Trading Systems (LETS), from the 'Thistles' in Ayrshire and the 'Hearts' in Birmingham to the Truro 'Talents' and the South Powys 'Beacons'. All of these initiatives are designed to boost the local economy by the matching of supply and demand in the area through barter and proxy currencies. In a similar vein, collaborative consumption is also on the rise, fuelled by the internet, with 'swap' sites like Freecycle helping the redistribution of unwanted goods; Airbnb and Parkatmy-House facilitating the commercial use of spare rooms and unoccupied drives; and car clubs and garden-sharing schemes putting to good use resources that would otherwise sit idle.

While these efforts – across the developing and the developed world, driven by commercial and by charitable aims – are noble and exciting, so much more could be done, were governments and the multilateral institutions to lend a visible hand to these entrepreneurial efforts, instead of leaving it to its invisible counterpart. While there will always be a concern about the potential for exploitation, or the propriety of 'first-world' intervention, arguably a key role of government and the multilateral institutions is to cast proxy 'votes' into the market for those who have no access, both domestically and internationally. If the state does not participate on their behalf, the dispossessed simply have no involvement, and barriers to their entry tend to increase not reduce over time as the market shapes itself to suit those who are able to take an active role.

Of course, it is also a toxic assumption to believe unswervingly in government intervention. Formally, this argument has been compellingly made by Stiglitz, who regards any economy characterized by government intervention as inefficient by definition, because the centralization of the ownership of large amounts of capital restricts the information that is the lifeblood of a healthy market to the civil service. This creates one of his 'asymmetries of information' and thus an imperfect market, one that undermines the whole motivation behind government intervention, which is to make the market more 'perfect' in order to benefit the maximum number of people. In this thinking, a freer market is likely to lead to better outcomes because it leverages the collective wisdom of everyone involved in the global marketplace by ensuring the free flow of information. Arguing from another angle, Ormerod has used non-linear signal processing to demonstrate the futility of intentioned government intervention in any case, arguing that the complexity of the system prevents clear feedback loops, so any notion of government control over the economy and society can only be 'illusory'. In his 1999 book *Butterfly Economics*, he notes that the most that can be expected in systems of such complexity is that behaviour can be mapped and explained – like rolls of dice – but not predicted to the level of safety that should be required by the state. He uses the example of the perennial Christmas toy fad to show that, in any case, consumer activity is actually more influential than government action. This is why government intervention is likely to be more successful if it is in the form of public policy as 'nudge' not push, so that the interventions are more about influence than control.

Whether they are designed to support innovation or enterprise, or to make the market fairer, what might such 'nudges' look like? 'Nudges' are those policies that, while not strictly speaking curtailing freedom of choice, nevertheless make it easier to choose one way rather than another, like changing organ donorship from an opt-in system (as in the UK, Germany and Greece) to an opt-out system (as in Sweden, Spain and Austria). Other examples would be the practice of labelling adjacent bins 'recycling' and 'landfill', or the Pennies charity, which helps retailers raise money for good causes by asking customers to round up their bill when they pay by card. In the UK, the Cabinet Office now has its own 'Nudge Unit' tasked with coming up with thoughtful 'choice architecture' to help improve national health and well-being. Such nudges might range from texting NHS appointment reminders to reduce non-attendance rates, or giving recipients the option to have their benefits paid weekly rather than monthly to assist with household budgeting. A recent nudge that proved successful in the UK was the introduction of alcohol gel throughout hospital facilities to encourage hand sanitation, which reduced the incidence of 'superbug' infections by 40 per cent in the space of a year. Other examples of nudges might be the use of mirrors in lifts to reduce graffiti, or the idea that reoffending could be reduced by stopping the release of offenders on

Fridays, just when many essential services, including those that cater for addictions, are about to close for the weekend. One crafty 'nudge' in the UK is the sign in the town of Telford that sets a speed restriction of 12 miles per hour. This rather precise figure means that motorists have to focus much harder on controlling their speed, improving local safety. In the US, research in Chicago showed that public safety can be improved by the simple nudge of planting trees and shrubs in housing developments, halving property and violent crime when compared with greenery-free concrete jungles.

Nudges might also be about smoothing the path, rather than just about influencing choice. For instance, the UK fair-trade organization Traidcraft has a policy designed to help their suppliers stay sustainable, which is to prefer those who have more than one crop or product to offer. When they wanted to assist Peruvian honey farmers, whose sole focus made them vulnerable, they encouraged them to expand into blueberries. Simultaneously, they launched a new Geo snack bar, using non-fair-trade American blueberries until the market for the new range was established, allowing a smooth and profitable transfer to Peruvian blueberries over time.

Also in the UK, the government supports charity shops with exemption from corporation tax on profits, a zero VAT rating on the sale of donated goods and 80 per cent mandatory non-domestic rate relief, funded by central government. A further 20 per cent rate relief is available at the discretion of local authorities. While many commentators have seen the replacement of empty shop units with charity shops as evidence of the collapse of the High Street, others argue that it assists footfall. Even if some of this is from the well-to-do middle classes in search of 'vintage' finds, such shops provide access to affordable clothing and other items, promote the recycling and reuse of unwanted goods, and offer valuable opportunities for retail work-experience through volunteering. While on one level this is not entirely altruistic - UK charity shops are reckoned to raise around £200m a year for a wide range of causes - the nudge provided by the tax break ensures their continued presence as a valuable option for those who find it hard to pay full price for expensive items like interview suits and work clothing.

More direct intervention by the UK government has often been packaged with health and welfare measures, including fluoride in tap water, the provision of free school milk for the under-fives, free school meals for poorer families, and 'meals on wheels' for the elderly. Many countries also mandate folic acid in flour. Like the modern commercial practice of bundling reduced gym membership fees with health insurance, these are designed to be health nudges, although it is not always clear how they really help to change behaviour or prevent larger health problems. Simply taxing sugar might do more for the nation's health than all of these measures combined. Recent moves to ban smoking in a range of public places, remove tobacco in shops and introduce minimum pricing for alcohol are further health-related nudges, the first of which has already had a significant impact.

It is harder to find examples of government nudges in the commercial sphere, except where regulation establishes a minimum wage or tax breaks for R&D, or where planning policy introduces quotas for low-cost housing. But one example where the government has intervened with a proxy vote to level the playing field for the UK poor is in the matter of banking. Noting the overwhelming business case for the electronic payment of benefits, the government was stymied in this regard by the fact that many benefit recipients did not have a bank account, often because they could not make it through a credit check. But the UK Post Office, whose footprint gives it the largest retail network in Britain, is state-owned, so the government decided that they should offer a universal bank service to allow all claimants access to a basic bank account. Sadly, this initiative was defeated on cost grounds, because none of the High Street banks would support it. But the nudge it provided did spur some eighteen financial institutions towards developing a basic bank account without an overdraft facility, which would avoid the need for a credit check that was unlikely to succeed.

Perhaps a contrary example might also help. In the UK, the benefit system financially disincentivizes the return to work of the jobless, as it also disincentivizes marriage and cohabitation where children are involved, because of the effect it has on payments. These nudges encourage unhelpful societal behaviour, particularly in communities suffering from inter-generational unemployment. Where there is no longer a culture of work, and the benefit system makes it financially more attractive not to bother, there is no shame in not working. This is in stark contrast to a scene in the 1997 British film, *The Full Monty*, in which a group of Sheffield steelworkers has been laid off. One of them, a former manager, is so ashamed he goes through the daily charade of donning his suit and setting out to work clutching his lunchbox, in order to avoid his wife finding out that he has lost his job. In *Moral Sentiments*, Adam Smith suggested that one of the chief reasons we are moral is because we feel held in the gaze of our fellow man, and we behave well because we want them to think well of us. This doesn't work, however, if we don't feel their gaze, or it is no longer likely to be critical. As well as addressing the financial barriers to rejoining the workforce, the UK government is also trying to address this problem of unhelpful nudges. While the unemployed no longer need to join the long queue at the Post Office on 'Giro Day' to get their benefit, payments now being made electronically, they do have to visit the Job Centre in person every other week to discuss their progress. This ritual is designed as a nudge - albeit one with only questionable success - without which the long-term unemployed would have no need to keep reviewing their situation. Much of the energy of the UK's Department for Work and Pensions is being spent trying to identify better policy nudges in this sphere, although the issue of the right sort of societal pressure is a hard nut to crack.

In the developing world, there are famous nudges like Trevor Baylis's clockwork radio to help communicate health messages about AIDS, and services and products like micro-finance, fair trade, and the solar-powered batteries mentioned above. Information being at a premium in many parts of the world, the UK government's current funding of the BBC World Service, which broadcasts in twenty-seven languages and reaches a weekly global audience of 166 million, is a popular nudge that tends to prove its particular worth whenever there is global unrest. Historically, the BBC's radio soap opera *The Archers* was devised by the BBC with the Ministry of Agriculture in 1951, as a way of encouraging farmers to try new techniques to increase productivity after the Second World War. Its success has been replicated in broadcasting throughout the developing world, from storylines encouraging sewing in Peru, establishing positive inter-caste relationships or promoting girls' rights in India, teaching sexual health in the Sudan, or how to avoid landmines in Afghanistan. Commercially, in Hindustan Unilever has introduced a shampoo that works best with cold water and is sold in small packets to reduce the barrier of up-front cost for the poor; recent moves by the company in London to develop washing powder that needs only small quantities of cold water to be effective will also be useful for communities where water is scarce.

Overall, however, the paucity of examples of high-quality nudges on behalf of those whose voice in the market is faint shows just how much work needs to be done. Relying on the toxic assumption of a non-existent 'invisible hand' will not deliver benevolent market outcomes. Neither will excessive state intervention in what is too complicated and fragile a system to be capable of being 'controlled' by regulation. It is of course far easier just to add new regulations to the statute books, or to remit the problem to the multilateral institutions for indefinite wrangling. It would take courage and considerable ingenuity to identify subtle ways to influence supply and demand on behalf of the poor both at home and abroad. While the efforts of the UK's 'Nudge Unit' are to be applauded, this kind of thinking needs to be much more widespread to have any real effect. It needs to be local, regional, national and global, and must involve governments, companies and charities. But the state's role is pivotal, and it can no longer be claimed that leaving the market to its own devices is a reasonable policy choice. Given that the 'invisible hand' will not deliver benevolent outcomes unaided, it is surely one of the state's central responsibilities to find ways to do so instead, and the world's strongest countries need to lead the way.

Chapter 3

The assumption of utility

One of the crowning achievements of the Enlightenment was the widespread adoption of utilitarianism – the idea that the aim of life is to seek outcomes that maximize happiness or 'utility' – and to deploy it as the basis for public policy. The idea that the good of an action is determined by its outcome appears entirely self-evident, and Jeremy Bentham's famous maxim of the 'greatest good for the greatest number' seems so wise that modern democracies are invariably built squarely on this ethic. Utilitarianism has proved particularly resilient as an ethical system because the system of law it produces can be shown to be generally in the public good, and citizens tend to understand the need for objectivity at state level. Neither is it formally associated with any particular religion, making it ideal for those Westernized countries who seek a secular state.

In *Moral Sentiments*, Smith himself talks of the two circumstances where moral reasoning kicks in: when we are about to act; and after we have acted. This logic produces the two traditional 'schools' of ethics: morality concerning the 'before'; and morality concerning the 'after'. A focus on forethought tends to favour the development of rules for living, and is usually called 'deontology'. Many religions have traditionally favoured this approach. In this ethic, right thought should lead to right action, and intention is all. Utilitarianism, in contrast, focuses on outcomes, and is often called the 'consequentialist' approach because it judges an act by its consequences, so a good end becomes more important than the means by which it is reached. Of course, predictions about likely outcomes can then be used to generate retrospective rules, uniting these two approaches, but rule-based utilitarianism retains its emphasis on the primacy of outcome over intention.

Perhaps it is easy to see why utilitarianism has become the pre-eminent public ethic. Morality concerning the 'before' tends to be about private motivation, whereas morality concerning the 'after' is about public behaviour. While a state may be interested in the former – largely for its preventative role – it is the latter that is more salient for community living. Because results tend to be public, there can be more discussion and potential agreement about the rights and wrongs of consequences than there can be about motives and what might have originally been intended. The current societal narrative privileges any approach that offers tangible measurement, because the dominant intellectual bias favours empiricism and the necessity of proof.

Adam Smith's friend, David Hume, was a famous proponent of empiricism, which is a type of philosophical scepticism of the kind characterized in the modern period by scientists such as Richard Dawkins. In Hume's *An Inquiry Concerning Human Understanding* of 1748 he described it thus:

> If we take into our hand any volume; of divinity or school metaphysics, for instance; let us ask, Does it contain any abstract reasoning concerning quantity or number? No. Does it contain any experimental reasoning concerning matter of fact and existence? No. Consign it then to the flames: For it can contain nothing but sophistry and illusion.

This highly rationalist favouring of 'number' and 'fact' made it inevitable that when economics gathered pace as a discipline in its own right, it would favour a mathematical approach. In an intellectual context where a good life – and therefore a good economy – was about 'maximizing utility', it did not take long for the 'utility function' to become the primary way in which economists modelled outcomes. Coupled with the Enlightenment ideal of man as a wholly rational, utility-seeking agent, 'Economic Man' was born, whose utility-seeking programming has been informing public policy ever since.

There are several critiques of utilitarianism, often focusing on the danger of ignoring motives or trying to guess the future. Perhaps the most devastating criticism strikes at the concept itself, by arguing that a goal of 'utility' is basically illusory. The theologian John Hughes has argued that at the heart of utilitarianism there is in fact an empty shrine. 'Pure' utility is an incoherent notion, because it begs the question: usefulness *for what*? And as soon as we try to peel away the onion layers to answer this question, we find that the concept is grounded by its instrumentality, unless we mobilize it towards a given end. It thus becomes self-referencing and circular, a trapped logic that can be used to justify almost anything, because all it does is protect our 'right' to maximize whatever our personal utility might be. On the face of it, this looks like a valuable human right that should be protected as a fundamental freedom. But using this as a *moral* system is disingenuous. As Aristotle expresses it, there is an important difference between *potentiality* and *actuality*. Using the example of language, he distinguishes between not knowing Greek, knowing Greek and speaking Greek. In the first instance the person involved is in a state of sheer potentiality. When they first learn Greek, they enter the stage of 'first actuality', in that they have realized their potential to learn the language. This first actuality, though, still constitutes a state of potentiality unless the person decides to exercise their rational powers and enter the 'second actuality' of speaking Greek. Perhaps there is even a subsequent stage, about speaking Greek well, or using the language to bless rather than curse. Enabling potential is in some ways a good in itself. However, the issue with making it the cornerstone of a public ethic is its amorality. An investment in enabling random potential does not necessarily harness it towards 'the good', or even the greatest good for the greatest number. This leaves the law to play catch-up whenever it goes the other way. Laissez-faire may be popular, but it allows the state to evade responsibility for one of its key roles as societal architect for the benefit of citizenry as a whole. As we have seen, allowing any sort of 'free market' to reign unfettered necessarily biases outcomes towards the strongest, and the state has a vital role as proxy, to protect those who might otherwise be overlooked.

But the toxicity of utility as an assumption isn't so much that it is a rather hollow and amoral concept, rather that it has attained an inappropriate monopoly. Its over-emphasis on the pragmatics of outcomes appeals objectively, but it fails to honour something deep in the human psyche, so it tends to run into public outrage at inconvenient moments. One example might be the universally negative reaction to the phone-tapping of various public figures by the media 'in the public interest', and a similar reaction to moves by the authorities to 'listen in' to electronic communication in order to pre-empt acts of terrorism. In both cases, philosophically speaking, the ends justify the means, but this does not mollify the public. Literature is full of illustrations of the folly of ignoring means in favour of ends because of its effect on the human psyche. For example, the plot of Dostoyevsky's

Crime and Punishment centres around the mental anguish of an impoverished ex-student who decides to murder an unscrupulous pawnbroker with an axe, on the utilitarian grounds that in doing so he could not only rid the world of an unscrupulous parasite, but also use her money to perform good deeds instead.

Utilitarianism also locks morality into a habit of thinking on a decision-by-decision basis, taking no larger view about ethics. As such, it is a perfect bedfellow for a world view that has tended to see the market as an accumulation of individual transactions, super-co-ordinated by a retro-fitted and benevolent 'invisible hand', but it is an incomplete narrative for the economy as a whole. 'Economic Man', that wholly rational utility-seeking machine, may be a useful device for mathematical modelling, but is not a particularly healthy reading of the nature of humanity. Indeed, its wide acceptance has led to further toxic assumptions, notably the presumed psychology underlying agency theory, as we will see.

But, leaving aside a negative casting of 'selfish' 'Economic Man', there are in any case a number of other problems with assuming that humans are wholly rational and that they are primarily interested in 'maximizing utility'. The first pertains both to individual behaviour and to the idea of utilitarianism as a whole, and it concerns the problem of 20:20 foresight. Economic models and public policy that assume outcomes are predictable should always be treated with suspicion when they involve humans and not machines. In economic theory this has become the classic confusion between what is called 'positive' and 'normative' economics. Positive economics is largely descriptive (eight out of ten cats prefer Whiskas), while normative economics is prescriptive (all cats should – or indeed will – prefer Whiskas), yet it has become the norm to confuse the two by assuming that what *is* ought also *to be*, hence the now familiar investment disclaimer that 'past performance is not a guide to future performance'. Many commentators worry that this habit – as well as being erroneous – leads to moral corrosion, as it tends to 'round down' to the lowest common denominator. If 'research' shows that most people lie, does it not follow that it is 'normal' to do so, and therefore no longer 'wrong'? The economist Donald Hay and many social psychologists argue that this kind of persistently deterministic thinking, particularly in a group context, naturally becomes suggestive. This is because it normalizes behaviours to the extent that fresh deliberation is seemingly no longer required, and thus 'everyone's doing it' becomes a universal justification. Apart from the obvious issue of the future being unknown, the idea that it can be confidently predicted through the past at worst denies humans their free will, and at best is a rather risky way to run society.

Perhaps this argument seems a little technical, given how used we are to using the past to predict the future. But there is another problem with assuming that we are all rational utility-seeking machines, given our human natures. The growth of behavioural economics is a response to the messy reality of human choosing and, as well as some Nobel Prizes, has produced many popular books with titles like *Predictably Irrational* that show our tendency towards sub-optimal decision-making behaviour. Apart from the fact that we can't predict the future, there are lots of reasons why we often don't choose to 'maximize our utility', none of which fit neatly into these kinds of mathematical models. These may be to do with altruism or reciprocity, but they may also be to do with faulty thinking. Aristotelian logic has produced a long list of 'fallacies' that cloud our judgement, like the classic 'slippery slope' argument – 'give them an inch and they'll take a mile' – often used to discourage the setting of a precedent that would seemingly trigger a chain of events. Perhaps you once had a teacher who told you off on the basis that 'what would happen if we all ran in the corridor?'.

A modern attempt to summarize how we mislead ourselves appears in the 2009 book *Think Again* by Ashridge's Andrew Campbell and his colleagues. They identify four 'red flags' that tend to be present in 'irrational' decisions. The first they call 'misleading experiences', when we are faced with a situation that appears familiar. In such cases, we assume that we know what to do, based on our previous experiences, and we deploy an old 'template' in a situation that is in fact new. Perhaps in the past we have always found that meeting up with an old friend is always fun, only to find that this time they have brought along a ghastly new partner, which means that in fact the evening turns out to have reduced our utility instead of enhancing it. Or perhaps we are only half-listening to someone, fast-forwarding because we think we know what they are going to say, and we make a decision that fails to recognize that circumstances have changed, like the boy who cried wolf. Often called 'jumping to conclusions', this flag is the habit of seeing two dots which look familiar, and immediately using them to draw a straight line before we have checked whether any of the other – newer – dots also line up.

A second red flag, 'misleading pre-judgements', occurs when our decision-making has been primed before we confront a particular issue by previous judgements or decisions we have made that connect with the current situation. Sometimes this is known as the 'sunk cost' fallacy, and characterized by aphorisms like 'in for a penny, in for a pound', 'might as well be hung for a sheep as a lamb' and 'throwing good money after bad'. Often, we have started down a path that we feel commits us to a given decision because we've gone too far to go back. This is what Macbeth meant when he said 'I am in blood stepped in so far that, should I wade no more, returning were as tedious as go o'er.' And once we hold any kind of prejudgement, we tend to indulge in 'confirmatory bias', selecting data to support our existing view rather than looking for data that might contradict it.

Their third red flag is 'inappropriate self-interest', which can be very powerful because it is often unconscious, and feels instinctive. It is the reason pharmaceutical companies persist in wooing doctors, and why advertising works. Because so much of our decision-making is subconscious, all the biases we wish we didn't have, such as those presented in Malcolm Gladwell's *Blink* on height, gender, race etc., as well as feelings about reciprocity, duty and how we think we will be perceived by others, all conspire in the blink of an eye to send us off in the wrong direction. The power of post hoc rationalization then allows us to make sense of our decisions, carefully editing out anything subconscious and self-interested. Of course, in some ways this is almost a definition of how 'Economic Man' is supposed to function, focusing on optimizing his own utility, but in this case the self-interest is inappropriate and weakens decision-making. Campbell's own example here arises from an analysis of the recent financial crisis, in which credit agencies widely underestimated the riskiness of the derivative products they rated. This misjudgement is widely held to have stemmed from unconscious and inappropriate self-interest, because the credit agencies were being paid for their ratings by the product issuers.

The fourth red flag is 'inappropriate attachments', such as the attachment we might feel to other people likely to be affected by our decision. Of course, to some people such attachments might feel highly appropriate, but the point here again is that *inappropriate* attachment clouds judgement by overly particularizing something that should properly be more objective. Favouring colleagues from a familiar part of the business in decisions over headcount, or short-listing candidates who have a recognizable or shared background, are common examples of this. Another would be the nostalgic retention of out-of-date company practices, brands or premises because of their historical links with the business, and often the personal career history of senior management. *Encyclopaedia Britannica*'s attachment to physical books has already been mentioned, and some commentators have criticized Nestlé for inappropriate attachment in retaining their much-disparaged infant formula business seemingly because it was the company's original product.

Other 'flags' not mentioned that are also considered to affect rational decision-making are largely contextual and linked to peer pressure. In 1972, Yale's Irving Janis introduced the concept of 'groupthink', which he defined as 'a mode of thinking that people engage in when they are deeply involved in a cohesive in-group, when the members' strivings for unanimity override their motivation to realistically appraise alternative courses of action'. He used this theory to explain the disastrous US invasion of the Bay of Pigs in 1961, and it has also been used to explain the NASA Challenger disaster of 1986 and the 2003 Iraq War. Groupthink leads to faulty decision-making when an overly homogenous and confident group becomes convinced of its invulnerability, and so tunes out dissenting voices in order to pursue a rigid, moralistic and often mistaken course of action. The pressure to conform is such that confirmatory bias becomes paramount, and the inevitable seniority of the group in question tends to discourage criticism until it is too late. This dynamic is often in play in criminal investigations when there is acute public pressure to solve high-profile murder or terror cases, and has been associated with a number of miscarriages of justice.

A related phenomenon is Art Kleiner's core group theory, where the thrall of the leader, or leadership group, makes followers pursue courses of action that they assume are desirable to the leadership but which may or may not find sanction in reality. Like iron filings clustering around the poles of a magnet, the psychology of followership means that staff will often conform to the imagined views of a version of their leader they have conjured up as a filter for decision-making. If the leader is remote, inscrutable or misunderstood, poor judgements will tend to result from this kind of well-meaning guesswork. Examples of this would be the sponsoring by the CSR department of a particular cultural institution that happens to include on its board of trustees a recently promoted senior executive, the coincidental introduction of generous healthcare provision by HR just when senior management starts needing it in earnest, or a telecoms company happening to fix connectivity in a remote area that is also a senior executive's favourite holiday spot. These types of contextual coercion shade into many of the red flags already identified, but are themselves a reminder of the relevance and potentially distorting effect of context, given that few decisions are made in a vacuum.

As a particular type of contextual influence, peer pressure in and of itself deserves a brief discussion. More properly, peer pressure tends to be the pressure we put on ourselves to conform to the real or assumed desires of our peers. While every parent has seen first-hand that from childhood we learn instinctively by copying, it was the French philosopher René Girard who formalized this as his theory of 'mimetic desire'. He argues that we learn what we want by seeing what our peers want, particularly those peers we aspire to emulate or attract. While core group theory talks about the distorting effect of leaders in this regard, Girard's theory draws the net more widely, suggesting that crowd behaviour in markets is a series of 'copyings' that scale up. Consumerism has turned this into a fine art by using 'role models' like David Beckham in advertising campaigns to accelerate this effect. And while there is something fundamentally rational about mimetic desire, most of the time it is unconscious. Because it is largely instinctive, its rationality depends on the rationality of the original actor, which will often be unknown.

A final nail in the coffin of our assumed rationality might well be that the ideal market, characterized by unlimited choice, also affects our ability to choose rationally. Columbia's Sheena Iyengar has conducted a famous jam experiment as a simple illustration of how too much choice actually paralyzes customers. In her experiment, she compared the behaviour of shoppers offered twenty-four jams to try, versus those offered just six. Both groups were given coupons for a subsequent purchase, but those exposed to the larger selection seemed confused by the array of options and tended to leave the shop empty-handed. A comparison across the groups showed that, while 30 per cent of those customers offered the smaller selection bought jam, only 3 per cent of those offered the larger selection did so. Too much choice can also trigger guilt and regret, because there are too many options to evaluate, and whenever research is conducted into what people regret most in life, the overwhelming finding is that people regret what they *haven't* chosen more than they lament a particular choice.

To recap, the Enlightenment arrival of utilitarianism on the scene as the dominant ethical narrative has been wildly successful in the building of modern democratic states. It does not suffer from deontology's identification with religious codes, and its focus on outcomes makes it ideal for public use. Its emphasis on the rational behaviour of human agents and its fit with scientific empiricism made it ideal as a founding idea for economics, such that utility has become the dominant model within the discipline. But, as we have seen, utility is an empty concept, and the idea that we are utility-maximizing automatons assumes too much in terms of human foresight and rational decision-making. But if this useful ethic that is also the cornerstone of economics is seen on closer examination to have a toxic whiff about it, how can it be rescued? One fruitful avenue of enquiry is the rebirth of the Aristotelian idea of virtue ethics.

Virtue ethics is often contrasted with rule or consequence-based ethics on the grounds that it is less about calculating the merits of individual decisions or transactions, and more about habits or underlying – and therefore more durable – character traits. If someone is in trouble, rule-based ethicists will help because they subscribe to a maxim that says the equivalent of 'do as you would be done by'. Consequentialists will help, because doing so will increase the utility of the person in trouble, and possibly their own in demonstrating their altruism. Virtue ethicists would help, because to do so would be the right thing to do, and would allow them to exercise the moral practice of benevolence. The argument may seem rather circular, in that character is built up over time and, as the cumulative effect of a series of decisions and behaviours, could in theory be informed by either a rule or consequence-based ethic. But the emphasis in virtue ethics is not about optimizing individual decision-making, it is about the development of moral character. As Aristotle himself puts it in his *Nicomachean Ethics*: 'we become just by doing what is just, temperate by doing what is temperate, and brave by doing brave deeds.' So it might be that, in pursuing this overall objective, an individual decision or two might not make sense in a one-off context, but make sense in the context of developing the right moral character. For example, having monitored the shift patterns of the local traffic wardens, normally I might calculate that if I park illegally ten minutes before a parking restriction lifts, I am unlikely to be caught but could maximize my own utility in terms of convenience and proximity. But if I am schooling myself in virtue, I might instead drive around the block, or park somewhere legal, in order to reinforce my habits of virtue, perhaps 'making a virtue' out of the walk back, too. The very British exhortation that one should do unpleasant things like play hockey in the rain because it is 'good for the character' is a case in point.

This focus on character emphasizes the development of morality over time, and so provides a long-term agenda for living an ethical life that is far richer than those offered by its competitor narratives. Rule-based ethicists would improve themselves by getting ever better at learning and interpreting rules, while diligent consequentialists hone their morality by becoming more skilled at reading the future in order to improve their ability to calculate outcomes. Both approaches are useful, but limited. Virtue ethics, in comparison, is a much harder discipline, because it requires a commitment to the development of a whole range of virtues, many of which may or may not see frequent use.

The American philosopher Robert Solomon explains the importance of this, in the context of dealing with the knotty problem of the findings of a variety of experiments that show humans in a very bad light. The most famous of these experiments are probably those conducted by the psychologist Stanley Milgram in the 1960s, and were designed to understand why, in the context of the Holocaust, so many people behaved so appallingly. The Milgram experiments involved a set of volunteers teaching word pairs to actors they thought were fellow volunteers. If the 'pupil' got an answer wrong, the 'teacher' had to administer an electric shock, with the voltage increasing in 15-volt increments for each wrong answer. The actors were issued with tape-recorded reactions (screams, etc.) and encouraged to bang on the wall and protest as the shocks increased, then to fall silent. In some versions of the experiment, the teacher was pre-warned that the pupil suffered from a heart condition. While many of the teachers did respond to these protests, and questioned the purpose of the experiment, most continued after being told firmly by the experimenter that they must go on, and that they would not be held responsible for their actions. The experiment was halted only if the teacher continued to question the experimenter after being told to continue four times, or when they had administered the maximum 450-volt shock three times in succession. In a poll conducted beforehand, Milgram established a general prediction that an average of just over 1 per cent of the 'teachers' would progress the experiments beyond a very strong shock. In fact, Milgram found that 65 per cent of the teachers administered the experiment's final massive 450-volt shock, even though many of them were clearly very uncomfortable about doing so, and every single one of them questioned the experiment at some point.

On the face of it, this shows a worrying capacity for cruelty. Solomon argues, however, that experiments like these serve to show in practice how hard it is to prioritize warring virtues, particularly if one is more 'supple' than the other. He sees it not as a lack of character in the 'teachers', but actually a conflict of character traits, a bit like the old sign outside a Boston pub that reads 'temperance in moderation'. In the Milgram experiments, the war was between the virtue of obedience to authority and the virtue of human compassion. In the average human life, there are many more opportunities to practise obedience to authority than there are to practise compassion, rendering this virtue commonly less supple than the virtue of obedience. This means that a virtue ethicist will be at pains to find opportunities to cultivate all of the virtues lest some become flabby with misuse and thus inoperable in practice. This proactivity is one key difference between a virtues approach and a rules- or outcomes-based morality, because these are by definition a reaction to a given situation or dilemma.

The latest thinking from neurobiology about the 'plasticity' of the brain would support the idea that virtue needs to be actively practiced in order for it to stick. It used to be assumed (yet another toxic assumption) that brain structure was largely fixed from childhood, and that our 'grey matter' degenerated with age. Neither of these assumptions now appears to be true. In fact, research suggests that older people don't so much forget things as stop paying attention in the first place, so that they fail to form retrievable memories. Similarly, while physical balance can degenerate, what is more common in old age is that *confidence* degenerates, such that older people take to wearing increasingly comfortable shoes and shuffling around. Because the brain contains numerous 'maps' to govern our functioning, draws and redraws them as maps that are not used tend to lapse. So, if the feet stop picking up information from the ground, the plastic brain stops updating its maps for walking and balance, until eventually the spare capacity gets colonized by another function of the brain, and the lack of balance becomes a self-fulfilling prophecy. This is the thinking behind advice about walking around the house in bare feet, and research that suggests that people living in towns with cobbled streets tend to be healthier, because walking on cobbles delivers the simultaneous benefits of free acupuncture and a brain workout.

According to this logic, if a virtue is not practiced, our 'map' for the virtue lapses. The development of moral character can therefore be seen as the acquisition of a skill just like any other. Virtue is a habit as well as an orientation, and virtue ethics is about developing the sort of character that leans towards virtue, until goodness becomes an instinct. Ethicists such as Matt Stichter have argued that the Dreyfus model of skill acquisition applies to the acquisition of virtue as much as it does to the learning of a craft. The Dreyfus model, commissioned to assist the US Air Force with emergency training, describes a series of levels. As the learner moves from Novice through Competence and Proficiency to Expert, they use rules, until these become principles, and finally intuitions, before they develop the kind of mastery that enables the kind of instinctively skilful behaviour that often rewrites the original rules. Another way to describe this process is the hoary old training favourite about moving from unconscious incompetence through conscious incompetence and conscious competence, to unconscious competence. It is only by persisting in the clunky process of crunching the gears and stalling that one day you turn up at work with no real memory of your drive there because you have been on autopilot.

Looking beyond the habits of Western systems of morality, the world contains a wide range of different solutions to the question of how best to live a good life, and what therefore should be the goal of society. The world's wisdom traditions, often preserved in religious writings, most commonly use stories rather than rules to communicate guidance about individual and communal living. These fables, parables, legends, myths, tales, proverbs and aphorisms often echo each other across the geographies, suggesting the existence of ancient shared narratives on matters like good and evil. These traditions all suggest a slightly more interested ethic than one which, like the economist's view of 'utility', privileges the individual's freedom over the common good. Equally, they all resist simplicity, often preserving for thousands of years deep ambiguities and contradictions, and few traditions favour a monolithic approach or one particular ethical school. This would seem to suggest that the neatness of utilitarianism and its current dominion is historically anomalous, and that messier systems like virtue ethics which are concerned with both means and ends, and with both the individual and society, are ultimately more likely to prove fruitful. As we discover more about brain plasticity, this need for constant puzzling makes more sense, as a vital discipline to keep our ethical maps fresh. Incidentally, this need for puzzling provides a much-needed argument to reverse the current trend of supporting the more applied educational disciplines to the detriment of disciplines like the arts and humanities. As the ethicist Nigel Biggar has argued, these disciplines have a vital role to play in moral formation and the teaching of 'choosing skills' because, unlike the more quantitative subjects, they require the development of sophisticated reasoning, and the ability to make compelling arguments about qualitative matters.

So our third toxic assumption, the idea that utility is the best way to measure both the effectiveness and morality of the market, can only really be justified if the 'invisible hand' exists. As we have seen, it does not. This renders utility an empty concept, because there is no guarantee that individual utility-maximization produces a good outcome overall. What looks deceptively neutral as a governing ethic then becomes colonized by the powerful, and thus a system based on utility cannot be effortlessly moral unless the powerful are universally benevolent. Additionally, a modelling fascination with utility has limited the efficacy of economics as an explanatory science, because it has largely ignored the messiness of human decision-making. While behavioural economics is making great strides, this is taking a while to translate into public policy. As we have seen, the psychology of choice need not stymie economics; rather it can rescue it as a vital tool for public policy through the careful design of nudges. But this debate needs to take place in a context that honours means as well as ends, and pays attention to moral hazard, in the context of the desirability of supporting the development of the virtues.

Chapter 4

The assumption of agency theory

In 2013, Marissa Mayer, the CEO of Yahoo!, created a media storm when she issued a memo that put an end to working from home by requiring all staff to be in the office. That a high-tech company could behave in such an old-school style attracted strong criticism, because it seemed to imply that staff could not be trusted not to 'skive' if they were not physically visible to management. This notion, that staff need to be actively supervised, is an example of a theory in economics called agency theory, or the 'principal–agent' problem. It is the idea that if a 'principal' hires an 'agent', they will struggle to align that agent's objectives with their own. The theory, based on Adam Smith's work, achieved particular prominence in the US in the 1970s, as economists struggled to advise manufacturing companies on how to maintain their competitiveness in an increasingly global marketplace. Agency theory assumes 'drag' from management, and so recommends strenuous efforts to force them to align themselves with the interests of the shareholders. A focus on 'shareholder value' – to which we shall return – was an inevitable consequence of this approach.

The landmark academic paper in this field was published by Michael Jensen (Harvard) and William Meckling (Rochester) in the *Journal of Financial Economics* in 1976. Their article opens with a quote from Smith's *Wealth of Nations*:

> The directors of such [joint-stock] companies, however, being the managers rather of other people's money than of their own, it cannot well be expected, that they should watch over it with the same anxious vigilance with which the partners in a private co-partnery frequently watch over their own. Like the stewards of a rich man, they are apt to consider attention to small matters as not for their master's honour, and very easily give themselves a dispensation from having it. Negligence and profusion, therefore, must always prevail, more or less, in the management of the affairs of such a company.

With Smith as their justification, the theory was formalized, and its wholesale acceptance has led to a whole host of policy and practice designed to align managers with shareholders, and workers with managers, and indeed anyone you hire to do something for you. Again, it seems so obvious that you would need to stand over your plumber to make sure he does the job properly that this assumption has gone largely unchallenged. But, under closer examination, this assumption is toxic. It assumes that people are naturally recalcitrant and have to be coerced. Most modern readings of the human psyche are actually more generous.

Psychology is a comparatively modern discipline. Of course, its antecedents are ancient, but in the modern period it can be summarized as the development of a series of three main approaches or schools of thought, each of which has achieved pre-eminence in turn, and all of which remain part of the discipline. Sigmund Freud (1856–1939) is widely seen as the founder of psychology through his creation of the discipline of psychoanalysis. Until he championed the 'talking cure', disorders we would now call psychological were usually considered to be physical ailments and treated accordingly. His understanding of the nature of the person remains famous, and has been preserved in several of the toxic assumptions we shall meet.

Freud founded the psychoanalytic school, key features of which concern the ideas of drive theory and ego psychology. In this world, our psyches are a battle between the childish id and the bossy super-ego, mediated by the sensible ego, and our lives are one long struggle to subdue our drives for things like food, sex and power, or to get them met without falling foul of the law. It is a world which is dominated by self-psychology and object relations theory, which holds that we are shaped by our preverbal relationships with objects, particularly our relationship with our mothers. This subjective experience of the self establishes our patterns of relating throughout the rest of our lives. Therapeutic interventions in this world focus on surfacing these largely unconscious drives, hence the emphasis on dreams, Freudian slips and the famous analyst's 'couch'.

A development of this school gave rise to the behavioural school of psychology. Probably the most famous example of this type of thinking concerns Pavlov's dogs, who were trained to respond when a bell rang and they were fed, and conditioned so that they ended up salivating upon hearing the bell whether or not food actually arrived. In this world, free will is illusory because all behaviour is determined by the environment. Freud's world is also one in which free will is negligible, but in his view we are driven from the inside, rather than the outside. For the behaviourists the environment provides a stimulus, which draws our response, in an iterative process that results in the formation of our particular character and psyche.

Part of this school looks specifically at the mental processes which support habit-forming behaviour, because thinking is widely presumed to precede action. The therapeutic intervention in this world, cognitive behavioural therapy, is the current NHS mental health policy of choice, and seeks to 're-programme' the brain with fresh scripts to drive better behaviour. Neurobiological findings about memory, habits and brain plasticity lend this approach strong support.

A departure from both of these rather gloomy worlds, where humanity is basically locked in a fight with fate, is the humanistic school. Influenced by existentialism and phenomenology and championed by Carl Rogers, in this world humans are innately good, and empathy, congruence and respect are the necessary preconditions for human flourishing. Included in this school is Gestalt theory, which encourages the practice of mindfulness and being fully present, and transactional analysis (TA), which uses Freud's ego states, and the idea of scripts from the behavioural school, to devise strategies that allow people to recover their self-efficacy. In this world, humans are not necessarily in need of therapy, unless they themselves want to 'expand' their life. Therapists in the humanistic tradition would tend to encourage this by focusing on the positive, and by encouraging their client - note not patient - to be self-directing. This school has itself developed a branch called transpersonal psychology, which seeks to take this core idea of the releasing of human potential further, into a more spiritual realm.

So, while modern thinking about the nature of the person borrows heavily from Freud, it has tended to move away from a largely negative and deterministic account of the human predicament towards one which sees the person as at least neutral if not positive, and emphasizes their freedom to act, or at least to choose not to be trapped by past experience. A new cloud on the horizon is the recent development in neurobiology that seems to suggest that our cognitive understanding of freedom may in fact rely more on 'physical' processing than has been recently thought, although these findings are as yet too new to determine their significance. It goes without saying that the debate about the precise nature of free will is an ancient one which could not be exhausted by any one research paper. And, whether your argument rests on religious belief or science, there has always been a tradition that fears we are all merely puppets, controlled by God or fate or biology or the environment to live out an essentially prescripted drama. Greek ideas about dualism and the evilness of matter, and religious ideas about original sin, support Freud's gloomy analysis. Together with many traditional ideas about parenting and schooling, agency theory appears to fit in with this worldview, and is designed as a remedy for the recalcitrance that will inevitably be shown by 'servants' or one's social inferiors in general.

And this view was popular in industry for a long time. The great Henry Ford famously kept a team to investigate his workers' lives outside the factory, and banned them from talking or smiling at work. Scientific management in the first half of the twentieth century, and the re-engineering fad in the second half, attempted to turn people into more efficient parts of an optimized machine. This logic, based on a rather negative underlying psychology, is best characterized by the popular 1960s McGregor Theory X and Theory Y idea of worker motivation. Theory X workers are exactly those to whom agency theory is addressed; they have to be coerced into work, and need constant supervision and discipline. Theory Y workers, on the other hand, are those recognizable from humanist psychology as being people who are inherently motivated, creative and responsible, and who need only to be given the right conditions in which to thrive. In the fields of organizational behaviour and human resource management, there has been a gradual move away from Theory X thinking towards Theory Y thinking. Some argue that this tracks the transition in the West to more professionalized service-based economies, and that Theory X is alive and well in the factories of China. This would tally with an analysis of motivation based on Maslow's hierarchy of needs, which suggests that people whose needs are more basic may well expect, accept and even respond more to X than to Y management. And some would argue that in any case many modern workplaces have lapsed back into Theory X thinking with regard to objectives, targets, performance-related pay and bonuses. This charge repays closer examination.

If agency theory encourages a rather gloomy view of humanity (or, at least, of employees), this is in turn reinforced by dated but persistent assumptions from psychology about the nature of the person. Nowhere is this better illustrated than in the torturous debate about 'managerialism'. Championed in 1981 by Alasdair MacIntyre's use of the Manager as a character in his seminal work, *After Virtue*, this concept reinforces the stereotype of the evil boss, and suggests that management is a cynical ploy to coerce and exploit the workers so that management may profit from their labour. While there is a long tradition, informed by Marx and upheld by the existence of trade unions, of 'management versus the workers', this effectively replicates a type of agency theory within organizations, as well as between them and the owners of capital, and is clearly influenced by Theory X-style thinking.

Managerialism is the belief, enshrined in the notion of an MBA, that generic management skills can be applied to all organizations, regardless of type or sector, and is used pejoratively by those who disagree that organizations share so many common traits. Those writing in this field identify a number of problems that find their home under this label, including the inappropriate use of private sector metrics in the public, professional, not-for-profit and faith-based sectors; the compromising of professional autonomy in the name of managerial control; and anything that smacks of 'too much management', with the mushrooming of public sector targets during the Blair administration in the UK being for many a particular example of managerialism run amok. MacIntyre himself pinpoints the core problem as being the commodification of the person and their subjugation to managerial 'technique' in the interests of efficiency. He sees the Manager as an amoral manipulator who treats organizational ends as given, and whose sole purpose is to bend recalcitrant workers to these ends through the tools of management. In the context of agency theory, this picture is intriguing, as it mirrors the implicit concern that shareholders are assumed to have about managers, while simultaneously reassuring investors that the company's executives will coerce the workforce into delivering the goods. It does therefore beg the question about what happens if the Manager were to use his techniques to his own ends and not those of the shareholders, and it institutionalizes a degree of organizational conflict that is at best inefficient.

This picture is rather extreme, but it does highlight the particularly key role of management, for good or ill. In 2000,

Fast Company magazine reported the findings of a new piece of research under the headline 'People Leave Managers, Not Jobs'. The research, published as a book in 1999 by Marcus Buckingham and Curt Coffman, was the write-up of two large Gallup surveys undertaken over a 25-year period, involving over 1 million employees and 80,000 managers from a broad range of companies, industries and countries. Their study identified twelve questions that measured the strength of a workplace, which were tested on a sample of over 105,000 employees from 2,500 business units across twenty-four companies, to find out whether in practice a strong workplace would equate to a more profitable workplace. The twelve questions, when answered positively, correlated with higher levels of productivity, profit, retention, and customer satisfaction:

1. Do you know what is expected of you at work?
2. Do you have the materials and equipment you need to do your work right?
3. At work, do you have the opportunity to do what you do best every day?
4. In the last seven days, have you received recognition or praise for doing good work?
5. Does your supervisor, or someone at work, seem to care about you as a person?
6. Is there someone at work who encourages your development?
7. At work, do your opinions seem to count?
8. Does the purpose of your organization make you feel your job is important?
9. Are your colleagues committed to doing quality work?
10. Do you have a best friend at work?

11 In the last six months, has someone at work talked to you about your progress?
12 In the last year, have you had opportunities at work to learn and grow?

As you can see from the list, most of the twelve questions essentially boil down to whether or not a manager shows an interest in their employees, and provides them with regular support and feedback. What was new about these findings was how overwhelmingly they suggested that employee satisfaction drives business performance, and that they identified the manager as the single most important influence on performance.

Few business schools now teach managers how to run Theory X organizations, except as a mode in crisis situations. Rather, 'leadership' today assumes a Theory Y approach, and is all about a humanistic quest to attract followers by offering them the right sort of vision, and by helping them to find meaning in their work. In doing so, leaders hope to charm their followers into giving the organization their wholehearted support, role-modelling loyalty and commitment for their junior colleagues. From the transpersonal school – the more spiritual version of humanism – organizational or workplace spirituality argues similarly, co-opting the religious idea of vocation for use in the secular sphere. Further, modern research into motivation continually finds that people are never more motivated than when they have the opportunity to do interesting work autonomously, and for which they receive managerial recognition and praise. Theory X indicators like pay and job security tend always to appear much lower down the list, although they remain of basic importance as hygiene factors, as would be formally argued by theorists like Maslow and Herzberg.

So, agency theory is doubly toxic, because it assumes friction between shareholders and management, and reinforces a similar assumption of friction between management and the workers. Both of these create inefficiency, affecting performance and ultimately return. But, as we have seen, this theory is based on a partial – and negative – reading of humanity. The evidence does suggest that managers have a crucial role to play, but for more 'humanistic' reasons than is commonly supposed. In playing this role well, management would naturally deliver better returns to shareholders by increasing productivity. The likely size of this gain is suggested by regular polls about levels of 'employee engagement'. Formally, staff are obliged only to deliver to their contract of employment; to do well, however, companies routinely rely on 'organizational citizenship' or 'discretionary effort' to get more out of their staff – behaviours such as altruism, loyalty, conscientiousness, an ability to work under pressure, thoughtfulness, attention to detail, and myriad others. They are the positive but not mandatory behaviours that make workplaces productive. But poll data on actual levels of engagement tends to be gloomy.

While these polls repeat at regular intervals, two polls from 2006 serve as typical illustrations of the genre. In the first, the Gallup Organization examined 23,910 business units and compared their financial performance with their engagement scores. They found that those with engagement scores in the bottom quartile averaged 31–51 per cent more employee turnover, 51 per cent more inventory shrinkage, and 62 per cent more accidents. Those with engagement scores in the top quartile averaged 18 per cent higher productivity, 12 per cent higher profitability, and 12 per cent higher customer advocacy. In subsequent research involving eighty-nine organizations,

Gallup also found that those in the top quartile for engagement enjoyed an earnings per share growth rate that was 2.6 times that of organizations with below-average engagement scores. In the second, Towers Perrin-ISR surveyed over 664,000 employees from fifty companies of varying sizes in a range of sectors around the world. Their survey reported that the operating income in companies with high levels of employee engagement improved 19.2 per cent over a twelve-month period, while the operating income of companies with low levels of employee engagement declined 32.7 per cent over the same period. Generally, such studies report that the average level of active engagement in a typical company is less than a third of employees, with the other two-thirds neutral or actively disengaged. This means that two-thirds of the workforce are likely to be doing the bare minimum. While companies by definition cannot demand discretionary effort, these figures suggest that poor management is leaving money on the table as concerns the productivity of the workforce.

Lest this should be seen as evidence in support of agency theory, the positive data reported above is instructive. So too is the index run by *The Sunday Times*, monitoring against the FTSE 100 the performance of those companies that make it into their Best Companies to Work For lists. This shows that companies that invest in their staff consistently outperform the market, and this trend has become more pronounced since the recession began in 2008, with returns now averaging more than four times that of the FTSE 100. There are plenty of examples, too, of spontaneous and productive creativity outside of work. In the UK, the Christian community alone contributes 23.2 million hours of voluntary service each month, over and above their church volunteering. Putting to one side the contribution of the vast armies of charity volunteers the world over, the existence of Wikipedia is also testament to the generosity of human endeavour. Launched in 2001, this free online multilingual encyclopaedia now has around 21 million articles, written collaboratively by a global team of volunteers. It has around 100,000 regular contributors, and is available in 285 languages. Another example is the recent crowdsourcing of computer-generated imagery for a new sci-fi series called *The New Kind*. This has been achieved by enlisting the help of an elite group of mentors and attracting the collective efforts of 200 anime enthusiasts scattered across the globe. These volunteers, identified through Facebook, YouTube and online forums, work in their spare time, sculpting 3D digital environments or adding effects, which are then blended together into the final product. UCLA has also harnessed the hobby time of 'the crowd', in designing a computer game to help identify malaria-infected blood cells. They have found that the crowd tends to get within 1.25 per cent of the accuracy of a pathologist performing the same task, helping eliminate the high cost and poor accuracy of diagnosis in areas like sub-Saharan Africa, where malaria accounts for one in five childhood deaths.

Some famously innovative companies have tried to mimic this kind of 'hobby' time within the core design of their jobs. The US manufacturer W. L. Gore allows staff 10 per cent discretionary time for their own projects, 3M has a similar '15 per cent rule', and the engineers at Google have 20 per cent of their time allocated for experimentation, which is reckoned to have netted the company 5 per cent of its new products since 2005. While Theory X-style thinking would assume such time would just be used for irrelevant time-wasting, this would appear not to be the result in practice. The Brazilian businessman Ricardo Semler, chairman of the conglomerate Semco, is famous for his democratic approach to work design, inspired by practices at W. L. Gore. He lets his employees set their own hours and their own salaries. They design their own workplace, and choose their own IT. Staff set their own production quotas, and everyone shares in profits. Every six months, bosses are evaluated by their subordinates, and the results are posted for everyone to read. Semco has an open-book policy, including the publication of salaries, and teaches factory workers to read accounts so they can understand the company's finances. This approach led to the growth in the organization's revenues from $4 million in 1982 to $212 million in 2003, and the company continues to thrive. Whether it is data from Gallup about engagement or the general perennial research on motivation, a common theme is that staff seek autonomy, challenge and meaning, for which they will repay an enlightened employer with high-quality work over and above the normal requirements of their job.

While agency theory does, as a consequence, suggest generic employee recalcitrance, the thrust of the theory is about a disconnect between shareholders and management. This is where most remedial effort has therefore been concentrated. But one pitfall of the widespread acceptance of agency theory is that it has actually become a self-fulfilling prophecy. Because of a concern that managers are not aligned to shareholders, most companies now include shares as part of the standard executive remuneration package. According to the economist William Lazonick, in 1992–5, 63 per cent of the average annual compensation of the 100 highest-paid US corporate executives came from the exercise of stock options and other share sales. By 1998–2001, this had increased to 79 per cent. It dropped back slightly between 2004–7 to 73 per cent but according to the corporate governance group GMI Ratings, by 2011 it had returned to a figure of 78 per cent. This represents a massive component of pay – ignoring bonuses – and depends on keeping the share price high. The effect? A formal merging of interests. In practice, it incentivizes management to inflate share price at the expense of investing for longer-term growth and value, thus institutionalizing the perceived conflict of interest. The widespread introduction of stock options as a core element of executive remuneration has contributed towards the massive increases in boardroom take-home pay relative to more junior staff. There is also a widely held suspicion that many executives, in their corporate role, use stock buy-backs to inflate the share price before they exercise their personal options, which would appear to be the agency theorist's worst nightmare, were such practices not simultaneously boosting the short-term value of the shareholder's holdings. In the UK, the Companies Act 2006 (Section 172) includes a statutory statement of directors' general duties which includes the requirement to 'promote the success of the company for the benefit of its shareholders as a whole' and 'to have regard to the likely consequences of any decision in the long term'. In spite of this, and even though case law is in favour of the board's role being primarily to safeguard the *long-term* interests of *all* of the shareholders, the collusion between opportunistic investors and stock-remunerated board members means that the short term inevitably wins out, which represents a massive but widespread collapse in governance, and a betrayal of the broader shareholding community. One caveat: not all companies are created for the long term. As Stefan Stern reports, research by

Deloitte estimates that in 1937 a business listed in the S&P 500 Index could have expected to spend 75 years in it. Today, the average is down to about fifteen years. But fifteen years is still a much longer time horizon than the end of the next quarter, or the cut-off date for annual bonus calculations, so this is no real excuse.

The effect of the stock option device, then, is to align the interests of managers with the interests not of the majority of shareholders, but with the percentage of them who are short-term and speculative investors. This would appear to be borne out by the actions of several companies during the 2012 round of annual general meetings (AGMs). Swiftly dubbed the 'shareholder spring' by the media, it started when over half of the shareholders at Citigroup and Aviva, and almost a third of the shareholders at Barclays, refused to back the board's remuneration plans. As more AGMs started to follow the same pattern, and three chief executives felt compelled to resign, companies started limiting shareholder attendance, with Duke Energy Corp and Bank of America using legislation intended for 'extraordinary events' to get official help with AGM policing in order to keep them out.

Senior management's regard for share price as a primary metric also drives a wedge between them and their junior colleagues, as investment in the organization takes second place to activities designed to attract the eye of City analysts. This means that senior management becomes increasingly isolated and myopic, focusing down ever closer on a small segment of the small amount of the balance sheet that is about the organization's historical financing. Their focus naturally becomes about managing the market, rather than managing the enterprise for which they are responsible.

Stock options are also widely held to incentivize risk-taking, because the value of a 'call' option increases with increased volatility. There is also no downside. If the risk-taking boosts share price, the option can be cashed in, but if the share price goes down, the option is simply not exercised. Admittedly, the reverse can also be true. If a risk might not play well at a time of year when the stock price needs to be high – perhaps because bonus payments are predicated on it – a management team may delay investments or announcements in order to manage volatility. Either way, management energy spent gaming share price is not energy spent managing the business, and a 2013 study by P Raghavendra Rau of the Cambridge Judge Business School showed that firms managed by highly paid CEOs experience lower future operating performance than their peers, particularly when this pay is in the form of stock options.

We will spend considerably more time discussing the folly of an obsession with share price but, at this stage, it seems that the toxicity of agency theory arises primarily from its status as an unproven 'fact', and the unforeseen consequences of executive shareholding as its most popular remedy. As we have seen, the theory assumes a theoretical but unproven recalcitrance which, as regards 'workers' in general, does not appear to be borne out by the facts – provided staff have good managers. However, the remedy of executive shareholding may well be working against itself, by distracting senior management from ensuring that excellent management actually happens. Without it, engagement levels fall, and Theory X-behaviour results. Data to link the staff engagement statistics quoted above with the remuneration arrangements of their bosses is hard to come by, but a negative correlation between senior executive stock options and general staff engagement might be a reasonable assumption to make.

Certainly, something is not quite working consistently for the shareholders with the current chief executive pay regime. Simon Patterson, of the remuneration consultancy Patterson Associates, has taken the total return to shareholders for a given company (dividends plus share price appreciation) and divided it by chief executives' total remuneration. Of those analysed, SAB Miller came top, with its chief executive returning £21,950 for every £1 he was paid. In second and third places respectively were Reckitt Benckiser (£11,598) and Diageo (£9,179). At the bottom of the league table were Legal & General (−£3,495), M&S (−£4,979) and Barclays (−£10,787). The worst by some way was RBS, where the figure was −£34,275, which means that, for every pound paid in remuneration to the chief executive, the shareholders as a group lost more than £34,000. The issue of pay and incentivization is a far larger one than can be deftly treated here, but would benefit from a more fundamental review as part of a larger investigation into the balance between returns to shareholders, longer-term company performance and the healthy distribution of profits.

Returning to agency theory proper, one perhaps controversial echo of it in the workplace is the fact that so many employees still depend on trade unions to fight their corner at work. Whatever else this is, it is evidence of a deep-seated culture that assumes a fundamental conflict of interest, such that the workers need representation to stop management colluding with the owners of capital to exploit them. Government statistics for the UK show that trade union membership levels reached their peak in 1979 and declined sharply through the 1980s and early 1990s before stabilizing. The current trend appears to be downward, however, as membership has declined over the last few years. Perhaps predictably, membership figures show that more junior than senior staff are unionized, and 5 per cent more women than men. Ethnicity data is mixed, although black employees are slightly more likely to join a union, as are employees who are disabled. A quarter of UK workers are members of a trade union. While capitalism reigned supreme in the twenty-year period between the fall of the Berlin Wall and the collapse in credit, these organizations seem to have struggled to identify a modern role. The intervening years saw a period of consolidation from which fewer but stronger trade unions have emerged, and current hardships have helped to give them a narrative. In general, though, they have been the dog that hasn't barked. While they offer many useful services to members, the trade unions and the Trades Union Congress urgently need to reinvent their place in the world of work, rather than hanging back and responding to events, or assuming that funding the Labour Party will be sufficient to achieve their goals. Some are already doing so, and a good example of agenda-setting has been the public sector union UNISON's lobbying about work–life balance. Were more unions to take a proactive approach to the work agenda, it would be harder for negative stories about them to be used to reinforce outdated myths about Theory X-behaviour.

But how could the core assumption about agency theory be unravelled to correct its toxicity? First, shares either need to be held by all staff or by none. The benefits of company structures that embed democratic employee ownership will be discussed later, but a first step to addressing the alignment of managers and investors would be to outlaw the practice of granting executive stock options, and require employees with private portfolios to declare their interest and details of any transactions made. Second, boards should stop guessing what their shareholders want and ask them. City analysts may want a frothy share price, but shareholding varies, and modern technology should make it comparatively easy to consult investors direct. Shareholders should not be the only party consulted, as we shall see, but their interest is still a legitimate one. One of the recommendations in the recent Ownership Commission report – to which we shall return – was the establishment of lobbying groups so that shareholders could achieve scale in their engagement with the companies in which they invest. Taken forward as a key recommendation of the 2012 Kay Review of the UK stock market, such an investor forum would certainly facilitate this kind of dialogue. Third, given the overwhelming evidence that good management boosts company performance, HR practices should measure this as standard in any performance management regime alongside 'harder' financial targets, and include this data in objective-setting and in reporting to stakeholders. Of course, there is no shortage of enlightened companies already leading the way in this field. But agency theory as a narrative has smuggled in such a negative view of the human being at work that more needs to be done to flush out those echoes of it that linger in the modern workplace.

Chapter 5

The assumption that market pricing is just

If you were to attend an MBA lecture on pricing, it would invariably be explained as an evolution from 'cost' pricing to 'market' pricing. As you might expect, cost pricing involves working out what it costs to create a good or service, and adding a margin to create a retail price. Market pricing is rather different, and is less about supply than about demand. Even if a plastic toy costs pence to make, if it is linked to a popular film or TV series, customers will pay substantially more than the cost price, so the art in this instance is guessing the maximum that the market will bear, or pegging the price to an associated product or service. Recent pricing theory has included the notions of premium pricing – the idea that some customers will pay way over the odds for a fashionable item largely because its expense renders it particularly exclusive – and predatory pricing, which is about charging less than an item actually costs as an investment in gaining market share.

Somewhere, lost in the middle of these simplistic categories, is an old debate about 'just' price. The mediaeval debate on this matter fizzled out with a consensus that the market price was probably just, because it was the point at which supply met demand. The idea of letting the market decide in this way tends to assume a degree of liquidity. If there is a large enough market in the product or service, multiple data points on supply and demand are generated, which average out at a reasonable and popular equilibrium. This makes the 'just' price a moot point if a market is dominated by a monopoly supplier, or by an oligopoly, a cartel or by government regulation. (There is a similar situation where the product or service is so new or rare that there is more room for manipulation, and it is harder to achieve a consensus on pricing.) Neither can this general rule, modelled on theoretical equilibria, take into account the essential messiness of pricing, which tends not to flex as much as the model would suggest, nor to be quite so democratic. But the theory is useful, because it serves as a reminder that modern pricing, with its bias towards demand, is more about information on supply and demand than it is about cost.

The notion of liquidity deserves a brief discussion. A market is liquid if there are lots of buyers and lots of sellers, such that an individual transaction will not disturb the prevailing equilibrium. Traditionally, economists have regarded liquidity as a good sign. Where something is rarely bought or sold, it is harder to establish a price for it. Conversely, if an item is frequently bought and sold, the multiple data points mentioned above are generated, producing a statistically more accurate average or range, and more price stability. This links back to the idea we've already met about the 'wisdom of the crowd'. In the earlier context, this was about how the 'invisible hand' could act as a metaphor for the order that arises from seemingly chaotic complex adaptive systems, such as those found in nature, or the economic system itself. The writer James Surowiecki wrote a book about this phenomenon, in which he offers a multitude of examples where the crowd has outperformed even the most brilliant individual. These range from the 'ask the audience' option on the TV programme *Who Wants to be a Millionaire?* to the Google search algorithm, which originally used data on web user behaviour to determine relevance in search results. He applies this thinking to stock prices and, controversially, comes out in favour of the much-criticized practice of short-selling. This is the practice whereby investors borrow stocks and sell them in the hope that the price will subsequently fall and they will be able to pocket the difference. Surowiecki reckons that short-selling isn't the scandal: the *lack* of short-selling is. This is because the feedback it embodies is as useful to the market as the more positive and opposite practice that assumes the health of a stock rather than its decline, because the 'wisdom of crowds' is flagging a problem with the company involved. Of course, he is careful to admit that crowds can still be victims of bias and herd behaviour, and subject to the 'red flags' and other flaws in rationality we have already met, as larger groups can sometimes magnify error rather than rounding it out. But he shows that, on average, a group will consistently come up with a better answer than any individual could provide. Like 'invisible hand' thinking, this is essentially the economist's argument in favour of liquidity, and the need for a free-floating price mechanism to convey the best information possible concerning supply and demand.

But toxicity in the area of pricing is based on two central confusions. One is that the price mechanism - allowing demand and supply to find a free equilibrium - automatically produces the 'right' price. The other is that pricing no longer has anything to do with the actual cost of providing the good or service. Let's take these in turn, starting with the idea that pricing is best left to the market. In his review of the financial crisis, Lord Turner, Chairman of the UK Financial Services Authority, ranked the proposition that market prices are good indicators of rationally evaluated economic value as top of his list of five 'intellectual assumptions' that the crisis had exposed as being flawed. But why is price mechanism theory toxic? Duke University's behavioural economist Dan Ariely explains that the fallacy on which it relies rests on the erroneous assumption, which makes sense in theory but not in practice, that supply and demand are independent variables. This suggests that the market price, the equilibrium between them, represents a 'scientific' resting point whose purity renders it unquestionable. In fact, supply and demand are much more iterative than this neat model would suggest. For example, Ariely has conducted a number of experiments to show how influenced demand is by supply-side suggestion, the immortal instruction of 'shampoo, rinse and repeat' being a particularly brilliant example of how to double demand. Leaving aside for the time being arguments about mimetic desire or copying, and that the fact that whole disciplines like marketing - and advertising in particular - depend exactly on this point, Ariely's modest experiments show how susceptible we are to anchoring and habit. This creates what he calls the idea of 'arbitrary coherence', which informs our decisions about what we will pay. Even something as simple and random as getting people to look at the last two digits of their social security number and then to state what they would pay for a variety of items has been show to act as an anchor and to skew 'logical' thought, as does an item's association with something for which a price - high or low - has already been established. This is of course the logic behind the 'positioning' of new products to take advantage of what the Nobel laureate Daniel Kahneman has famously dubbed the 'anchoring and adjustment' bias. This explains why we tend to pay more for products or services in some contexts than others, like a cup of tea in an exclusive hotel as opposed to a roadside cafe. Then, a precedent having been established, we tend to repeat our behaviour in a given context until it becomes a habit.

The diamond market is a case in point. In the 1940s, De Beers, sitting on a glut of diamonds, created an extraordinary luxury market for them with an advertising campaign now so famous that *Advertising Age* has named it the advertising slogan of the twentieth century: 'A Diamond Is Forever.' Before this date, other stones were considered more precious or romantic. Now, De Beers was urging men to demonstrate the durability and brilliance of their love by spending at least a month's salary – two months' in the US, or three in Japan – on a diamond engagement ring, which their wives should then keep for posterity, as a family heirloom. With the price set high, and the second-hand market stifled by such items' sentimental value, De Beers could control the supply and price of about 80 per cent of the world's diamonds, as well as influencing demand through emotionally devastating advertising: you can't really mean it if you don't buy her a diamond. Reinforcement in the 1950s through Marilyn Monroe's famous rendition of 'Diamonds Are a Girl's Best Friend', and Ian Fleming's choice of title for the fourth 007 book *Diamonds are Forever*, only helped to cement this positioning. Every year, 1.7 million American couples buy a diamond engagement ring. The US market for diamond engagement rings is estimated at around $4.5billion, which does not include separate campaigns about eternity rings (again, a diamond is forever) or 'right-hand rings' for self-made women. Unlike traditional safe-haven luxury commodities, diamonds do not go up in value unless a particular stone is connected with royalty or Hollywood, and, like new cars, they tend to have a resale value of less than

50 per cent of their original purchase price. And, contrary to the mythology, diamonds are not rare; supply is just tightly controlled. Indeed, jewellery diamonds would fetch a price of between only $2 and $30 if repurposed for industrial use. The diamond industry is not alone in using influence over both supply and demand to keep prices high, but it is a good case study for the toxicity of the assumption of the clinical neutrality of 'market price' given this industry's connections with corrupt regimes, exploitation and human tragedy.

The advent of the internet has facilitated some interesting experiments on pricing, the most famous of which is the 'perfect market' of eBay, which we've already encountered as an example of 'pure' capitalism in practice. Sites like eBay provide a platform for sellers and buyers to agree prices through an auction, although over time sellers have tended to set a minimum reserve and/or a 'buy it now' price which slightly muddies the water. Research carried out in 2000 by a team in the economics faculty at Vanderbilt University looked at over 20,000 auctions of Indian-head pennies during July and August 1999 and mined the data for patterns. This was supplemented by the detailed analysis of a sample of 461 mint-condition Indian-head pennies, for which accurate estimates of book value had been obtained from a coin collector. This research showed first that a seller's feedback rating, as reported by other eBay users, had a measurable effect on auction prices, with negative feedback having a much greater effect than positive feedback ratings. Second, the practice of setting a minimum bid or reserve price tended to have a positive effect on the final auction price, although in setting this floor the seller risked a non-sale. Third, if a seller chose to extend the auction to last for a longer time period, this on average significantly increased the auction price. While game theory explains these findings - more information communicated through the ratings, which act as a proxy shadow of the future, and a longer process to observe the behaviour of fellow-bidders - as well as the use of minimum pricing that Kahneman would recognise as anchoring, ultimately this research shows that even 'perfect' markets like eBay can be gamed in order to boost prices.

The other toxic assumption about pricing is the drift towards market-based pricing, and its consequent dislocation from underlying costs. This has proved problematic, because it has slowed down the mainstreaming of an otherwise useful development in pricing theory, namely the nascent debate on 'externalities'. The typical economics undergraduate soon gets acquainted with the 'free-rider' problem. As its name suggests, the problem examines the effect of too many people taking a free ride on public transport, as translated into any sphere where someone consumes a resource without paying for it. If no one paid, the buses couldn't run, just as if no one paid taxes, public services could not operate. In this context, a debate has arisen about the extent to which businesses are 'free-riding' on public goods, and are consuming them without making any contribution to their upkeep. These have been referred to as 'externalities' and are a modern attempt to express what the economist Karl Polanyi called in the 1940s the market's social 'embeddedness'. Pricing these externalities back in is designed to get round the free-rider problem as regards use of public goods, as well as to make these costs explicit to facilitate comparison and measurement. As an example, the International Center for Technology Assessment in Washington DC has looked at the total cost of gasoline, adding back in costs associated with climate change, oil industry tax breaks, military protection of the oil supply, oil industry subsidies, oil spills, and treatment of car exhaust-related respiratory illnesses, and reckons this at $12 a gallon, on top of the customary US $3 price tag, giving a 'real' cost of $15 a gallon.

One particular version of the free-rider problem is the so-called 'Tragedy of the Commons', the title of a famous paper written by the ecologist Garrett Hardin and published in the journal *Science* in 1968. A 'tragedy of the commons' occurs when multiple individuals, acting independently in their own self-interest, as recommended by Smith, ultimately deplete a shared limited resource, even when it is clearly not in anyone's long-term interest for this to happen. A famous example of this is the collapse of the cod fishing industry in Newfoundland, which led to the 1992 decision by Canada to impose an indefinite moratorium on fishing in the Grand Banks. While this is in itself an example of the 'invisible hand' delivering the opposite of a benevolent outcome, it also shows the dangers of not costing in externalities, so that the cost remains hidden until it is too late for the 'common' to be rescued. Some have argued that morality as a social good is relied on by markets but tends to be eroded by them, and is subject to a tragedy of the commons in the same way. For example, numerous studies by academics such as Wharton's Adam Grant have shown that exposure to an education in economics reduces ethical decision-making over time. When pricing is more about what the market will bear than about cost, these kinds of debates are easily overlooked, and externalities have to be priced back in instead through unpopular and compulsory government taxes, levies or fines.

In vogue at the moment is the pricing back in of costs arising from pollution by the levying of carbon taxes, or by imposing 'cap and trade' schemes. Most of the original schemes did this by allocating 'free' permits, hoping that a healthy secondary market would result, so that those with good habits could make money selling their excess permits to those lagging behind. But when the permits are traded, they are so cheap that they now just get factored in as an additional business cost, so the success of such schemes in changing polluter behaviour is questionable. In his 2009 Reith Lectures, Harvard's Michael Sandel used the example of childcare fines to explain this conflict between 'fines' and 'fees'. When nurseries imposed fines for the late pick-up of children, they found that late pick-ups actually increased. This was because parents started treating the fine as if it were a fee. Because it was worth more to them to be late than to incur this additional childcare cost, they simply factored it in. But as Sandel points out, fines are supposed to register moral disapproval in order to discourage unwanted behaviour, whereas fees are simply prices that imply no moral judgement and will just become a cost of doing business. This, then, is a central tension in the pricing back in of externalities, because the idea behind initiatives like carbon trading is actually to discourage bad behaviour. That money may also be raised is secondary, although it can be useful to finance corrective projects. So, the policy challenge is not only to get the pricing right, but also to be careful that the process does not create moral hazard by removing the incentive for organizations to improve negative behaviours, such as polluting, over the longer term. More widely, the externalities debate argues for a much broader understanding of the 'business case' for key policy decisions. On a narrow view, it made sense to close Britain's failing coal mines in the 1980s, but the long-term second-generation implications for communities dependent on the pits for employment have been severe and costly. Saving money from one part of the government's balance sheet, as has been the case with the restructuring of many other subsidized industries, merely moves the cost to another part of the government's balance sheet in benefit payments and other associated health and regeneration costs. The total cost of such decisions needs to take into account the broader societal picture, both in public policy and in private enterprise, lest the conditions necessary for economic flourishing go the way of the Newfoundland cod-fishing industry.

As well as cloaking the debate on externalities, another casualty of the price mechanism has been interest, which is now merely the price of money and as such has become subject to the same pressures on pricing. The practice of charging for money was traditionally called 'usury' and used to be anathema. A horror of usury stems from the Aristotelian view that it is 'unnatural' for sterile money to breed money, so money should not be lent out at interest. The world's three monotheistic religions all contain a formal prohibition on lending at interest. Over time, their positions have been finessed. Famously, Jewish interpretation qualified the ban to limit it to fellow Jews, releasing Jews to become the money-lenders of Europe. The Christian Scholastics qualified their own ban to allow the calculation of the opportunity cost of forgoing use of the money lent, and the risk of it not being repaid, to give an amount of 'compensation' that was effectively 'reasonable interest'. Over the years, usury was repositioned as a term to refer to 'unreasonable' levels of interest, rather than to interest itself, as was reflected in the existence in law of interest ceilings. For example, English legislation in 1571 distinguished between usury and interest, legalizing the latter to a ceiling of 10 per cent. Usury laws of various kinds remained in force in places like the US until as late as the 1980s.

As an aside, Islam continues to observe an outright ban on interest. Shariah-compliant financing avoids it by creating financial instruments that render loans either as leases, or as investments that attract profits – or losses – in lieu of interest. In 2005, 'zero-interest banking' as a sector was estimated already to have reached the $500 billion mark internationally, and to be growing by at least 10 per cent a year. The equivalent of a 'mortgage' involves the lease of an asset, e.g., a house, to a customer for an agreed term in exchange for fixed rental payments, with the option to own the asset at the end of the term. Similarly, halal capital funding is provided to businesses and entrepreneurs in exchange for a share of profits. The provider of the capital bears any losses incurred, unless the entrepreneur involved can be shown to have been in breach of contract.

In a world where physical coinage was still the most common form of currency, it is perhaps easy to understand Aristotle's rather literal view about interest. In a world where a plastic card or a typed-in code is the most common way to transact a purchase, however, matters are less evidently simple. Indeed, 'money' means something entirely different these days. Tracking its evolution starts with the first people meeting to barter goods and services. Before long, it becomes apparent that some kind of secondary system would make this primary market more efficient – what if I want rice today but will only have the corn to swap for it tomorrow? So different cultures start using different 'stores of value' – cocoa beans, glass beads, camels, metal discs – anything that that community feels has the right sort of intrinsic value to represent the price of the materials being traded. Over time, coins became the most common tools used in market transactions, and originally were worth, in the amount of precious metal they contained, exactly the same amount as the amount stamped on them.

But once this system was established, it became clear that people didn't feel the need to melt their coins down to extract their absolute value all the time, and were happy to use them as tokens. Modern coins have very little intrinsic material value, and coins themselves soon gave way to notes as a more convenient way of transporting buying power. These promissory notes were often banknotes but could be any kind of IOU – a cheque, a certificate, a plastic disc, or any token that both parties agreed held validity as a deposit or guarantee of ultimate payment. Interestingly, the reduction in use of physical money has had some positive side-effects. For example, according to the Bank for International Settlements, notes and coins are used in about 9 per cent of eurozone transactions and 7 per cent of US transactions, but in only 3 per cent of Swedish transactions, and this is already having an impact on Swedish crime statistics. For instance, the number of bank robberies in Sweden dropped from 110 in 2008 to only 16 in 2011, and the number of robberies from security transport is also down. It is also likely that societies migrating towards a more virtual system avoid the problems of bribery and corruption that largely depend on a cash economy, although of course electronic payment carries its own risks.

In parallel with these changes in the etiquette of purchase, the banking system also changed. Instead of banks literally holding the entire value of deposits made with them, they realized that they could lend quite a lot of this out, given that in practice people seldom needed regular access to their money.

So fractional reserve banking was born, and banks ever since have played the odds on lending out as much as they can, while retaining just enough hard cash in their vaults to pay back anyone who wants to reclaim their deposits. For example, the average cash reserve ratio across the entire UK banking system is estimated to average around 3 per cent. This is to become a statutory target by 2015, in preparation for global convergence in 2018 under the Basel III accord. In the US, where reserve requirements are already regulated, the ratio ranges from 3 to 10 per cent, depending on total size of holdings. But neither of these ratios gives much scope should depositors become nervous. Nowadays, the idea that you can lend out - or borrow against - assets that are not actually yours has reached monumentally sophisticated proportions in the financial markets, with everyone hoping that when the music stops someone else will be left without a chair. Of course, credit - the idea of delaying payment - would have been used even in a barter economy, where one party promised a given product tomorrow in return for another one today 'on tick'. But nowadays credit is treated as a currency in its own right, with the advent of the ubiquitous credit card.

Thus, modern 'money' has essentially become information about relative value, and about supply and demand, and currency itself has become a commodity like any other. As we saw in the discussion on pricing, that someone can buy a Mulberry handbag for £4,000 doesn't mean the bag 'costs' £4,000, but that there are sufficient people with enough disposable income to pay this amount to own something that few other people can afford to buy. Similarly, footballers' or chief executives' salaries are no longer about what a person is 'worth' but about what the market is prepared to pay for exclusivity. And it is this market in information about relative values that drives so-called 'casino capitalism' where positions are taken on where supply and demand will move across a huge range of asset classes, as well as positions on those positions, and positions on the positions of those positions, and so on. While this hedging or insuring of 'real' assets through secondary and tertiary mechanisms – securitization – is designed to protect the original asset, nowadays separate markets have developed to trade these positions in their own right. And the sophistication of modern computing means that multiple transactions can be executed in fractions of seconds to take advantage of infinitesimal changes in prices. In order to speed up financial transactions by 6 milliseconds, a $300 million, 3,741 mile underwater cable is currently being laid between London and New York, because each millisecond saved is estimated to boost a hedge fund's annual bottom line by $100 million.

At each stage in the evolution of 'money', increasing amounts of trust have become a condition of operating in the market. In the original markets, a customer could physically examine the carrots on offer, or check whether there were weights hidden in a sack of corn. But coins rely on a stable administration, and IOUs require trust that a debtor will come good. The public needs to trust the banks to give them their money back on demand, and it is when this trust breaks down that queues gather outside the likes of Northern Rock, or governments call on banks to 'recapitalize' in order to reassure the public that they actually own at least a nominal percentage of what they owe. And the credit crunch of 2008 happened because the banks stopped trusting each other about the statements they were making about their exposure to bad debt. So if money, and market transactions, are now essentially about trust, the Occupy tents that appeared in Wall Street and outside St Paul's in London, not to mention the backlash over bank bonuses, should have made the bankers and politicians a lot more worried than they appeared to be. In any case, that money, as a commodity, has a price like everything else is now broadly accepted. And, as with pricing in general, the use of market-led pricing removes any sense of ceiling, leading to as much outrage over the 5,853 per cent APR charged by Wonga – or even the comparatively modest 545 per cent APR charged by Provident Financial – as there is on spiralling boardroom pay.

Now that global currency trading has made money more obviously comparable between different nations, it may not be useful to reopen the debate about whether money should or should not be treated as a commodity, or traded. Otherwise, it would be a candidate for another toxic assumption. But if pricing – albeit flawed – is essentially about the expression of relative values and an indication of supply and demand, it would not make sense to 'un-invent' this trade. However, like any innovation that has questionable ethical outcomes, it should still be possible for governments to reach decisions on when the price of money should essentially be set, in the public interest, as is currently the case with official interest rates. Payday lending is one such area where a reintroduction of some sort of usury law would protect the weakest in society and stop them entering a spiral of debt with its associated wider social consequences.

The price mechanism, then, is not as innocent as it appears, and an unquestioning faith in it is our fifth toxic assumption. This is because the market mechanism assumes the independence of supply and demand, which we have seen is not true. Further, adherence to market pricing as an absolute principal masks an important debate about externalities, threatening the long-term health of the economy through tragedies of the commons. While money is a special case, it may be that more intervention is needed to agree 'just prices' where not doing so would lead to unwelcome societal consequences. National interest rates are already established, as are prices like the minimum wage, and many would argue for a maximum wage, or wage ratio, too. In any case, the consumer should no longer allow themselves to be fobbed off with prices they feel are too high, on the basis that they are 'market prices' and so somehow divinely ordained. The 'pay what you want' phenomenon is offering an interesting challenge to traditional pricing, popularized by the band Radiohead's release of their album *In Rainbows* for digital download, where customers chose to pay an average price of £4. In the first year, it sold over 3 million copies. Because price is about information, the more consumers flex their muscles by sharing their experiences, complaining, and asking difficult questions about costs, the more companies will have to compromise in order to protect their wider reputation. Consumer groups already perform this function, but it is hard for them to gain traction while society is in thrall to a mantra about the inviolability of the price mechanism. Supply and demand are inter-dependent variables, so an active customer lobby can do as much to affect prices as those who set them.

Chapter 6

The assumption of the supremacy of the shareholder

One iconic story of a modern business start-up, which heralded the birth of Silicon Valley, was the classic 'two blokes in a garage' story of Hewlett-Packard. In 1939, Bill Hewlett and Dave Packard established Hewlett-Packard (HP) in Packard's garage in Palo Alto, with an initial capital investment of around $500. They struck lucky winning an early contract from Walt Disney and moved out of the garage, incorporating in 1947. Ten years later, HP went public, to help with estate planning for its founders, and to enable employees to share in the company. The shares sold for $16, and the float financed new offices, an acquisition, and overseas expansion. After a series of inventions, acquisitions, de-mergers, and a merger with Compaq, HP is now the world's largest IT company, with annual revenues in the region of $127 billion. This fairly typical account shows how share-ownership tends to work. Companies are usually started with private or loan capital, or by attracting partners willing to invest money in exchange for a share in the business. When they achieve the sort of scale that needs a serious injection of cash, they will tend to float on the stock market. This Initial Public Offering (IPO) might also be an opportunity to reward the original investors for their commitment. Equally, an established business might want additional funds to finance expansion, so might ask existing or new partners to provide fresh funds in exchange for shares. Companies may then return to the market periodically for more funds, and each time they acquire, merge or de-merge, the nature of the shareholding changes. Invariably, their 'founder' shareholders may die, or wish to pass on their share to another party. This creates a market for the original shares, which attracts individuals or institutions that reckon a share in this particular enterprise will allow them to share in that enterprise's future profits. Traditionally, shares were acquired not so much for their gradual appreciation in face value over the long-term, but for the regular dividend income they provided, which turned them into a type of annuity. This made an equity portfolio ideal to finance regular living expenses, or as part of pension planning. Regardless of their status or reasons for investing, 'the shareholder' has become central to the company narrative.

The Nobel laureate Milton Friedman, scion of the Chicago School of Economics and arguably the most influential modern economist since John Maynard Keynes, famously claimed that 'the business of business is business' and that its leaders have no social responsibility 'other than to maximize profits for the shareholders'. This thinking seemingly entered the bloodstream through two articles in the *Journal of Law and Economics* in 1983, co-authored by Eugene Fama of the University of Chicago and Michael Jensen of the University of Rochester (New York). Building on Jensen's earlier work on agency theory, they argued that a focus on 'maximizing shareholder value' would deliver superior economic performance, and so corporate resources should be allocated to maximize returns to shareholders because they were the only economic actors who make investments without a guaranteed return. The widespread adoption of this mantra of 'shareholder value' crowns the shareholder supreme, and its pre-eminence as a corporate objective is a direct consequence of widespread acceptance of agency theory. Positioning the shareholders as the principals and the organization's employees as their agents in order to make the argument about a 'principal–agent problem' smuggles in the assumption that this is a correct analysis of their respective roles. And once this has been accepted, what better remedy than to 'cure' the conflict of interest by devising strategies to deliver shareholder value, as the *raison d'être* of organizational life. In step with the increasingly accepted orthodoxy of agency theory, technical and regulatory advances also made equity trading a more attractive way to generate a return, and contemporary changes in legislation created the modern 'professional' institutional investor. Together, these developments fundamentally changed the culture of shareholding, which had necessarily been a longer-term undertaking in previous times.

This refocusing of strategic attention to laser in on shareholder value - widely endorsed by Reagan/Thatcherite policy in the 1980s - is what Lazonick has called the seismic shift from 'retain and reinvest' to 'downsize and distribute'. There is an argument from efficiency that freeing up money to be recycled back into the economy via a focus on shareholder payouts is helpful, particularly where mature businesses may have less need to reinvest for growth. The new class of institutional investor, under pressure to produce returns, would have been more than happy to accept this thinking. Under a regime of 'downsize and redistribute', management's focus is on improving the return on equity by cutting costs, often through reducing the size of the labour force, and returning the spare cash to shareholders.

Meanwhile, the growth of the market in securitization, to protect these underlying investments, has added to the pressure for equities to produce a more immediately evident yield. And once a precedent for yield has been set, whether through dividend payment or just increased share price, investors build an assumption of annual growth into their projections, punishing the organization if it departs from this pattern in the future. Indeed, the academic Stephen Chen has used modelling to analyse fraud, showing that it is this shareholder expectation of compound growth, more than CEO character or any other contributory factor, that provides conditions ripe for financial misreporting. Each year, growth sets a new baseline and a new expectation, rendering 'ordinary' growth disappointing, and triggering a collapse in the share price. Additionally, a paper written by the American academics Bartov, Givoly and Hayn shows that it is now more profitable for chief executives to manage expectations, rather than actual business performance. Indeed, they found that a company's stock will perform better if it earns £1 a share against an expectation of 98p, than if it earns £1.05 against an expectation of £1.08 a share. While it may be intuitive that exceeding expectations is always a more popular move than disappointing them, in this context there is a risk of translation into a dangerous strategy that prioritises spin over substance. This is what the Canadian academic Roger Martin has called a single-minded focus on the 'expectations market' rather than the 'real market', which incentivizes boards to be increasingly remote from the businesses they are charged with managing.

Whether or not companies do misreport or focus unduly on perception over reality, these findings show what tremendous pressure is brought to bear by the 'shareholder value' approach.

Managing corporate performance through this lens becomes an infinite treadmill, where boards are under permanent pressure to improve it to the exclusion of any other metric. Because of its simplicity and ready availability, both the institutional investor and automated trading use share price as the primary performance metric, so it is no wonder that the modern chief executive monitors this daily, agonizing over every dip, rejoicing over every lift and employing sophisticated PR manoeuvres to try to keep it buoyant. This paranoia and short-termism is compounded by the modern practice of rewarding senior management with shares and stock options, ostensibly to align their interests with shareholders to solve the agency problem, which has also institutionalized the 'downsize and distribute' approach. So not only are managers furiously husbanding share price for the shareholders, they are doing so on their own account as well, with all the attendant dilemmas of 'insider dealing'. As Andy Haldane reports, at the peak of the boom, the wealth of the average US bank CEO increased by $24 for every $1,000 created for shareholders, and they earned themselves $1 million for every 1 per cent rise they were able to create in the value of their bank.

We have already looked at why executive shareholding can skew decision-making, in the discussion on agency theory. Whatever else it does, it drives a wedge between those running the business and those running the share price, which may be related but are quite separate things. But management by share price is toxic and foolhardy for two reasons.

First, it is highly susceptible to analyst whimsy, rumour and conjecture. Second, it is measurement by proxy. Both of these reasons make it too error-prone to be a reliable primary dashboard metric. Stories to illustrate this first point appear every day. A recent one involved a report in the UK *Mail on Sunday* that the bank Société Générale was in a 'perilous state' and on the 'brink of disaster'. The bank's shares fell 8.4 per cent the day after the article was published, so SocGen sued, and was awarded substantial damages in compensation, with the *Mail* being forced to admit that its story was not true.

Second, the matter of measurement by proxy. In the debate about excessive managerialism, one of the critics' most common charges is a habit of inappropriate measurement. Whatever is measured becomes what is managed, leading to unfavourable newspaper headlines when hospitals cut waiting times by using corridor trolleys, universities 'borrow' academics to get them through the research assessment exercise, or schools suspend all teaching other than on SATs in an attempt to boost their position in the league tables. Even in industry, the dawn of employee objectives has caused such a side-effect, driving behaviour which is narrowly focused on achieving just those stated objectives rather than any wider good for the organization. Indeed, the term 'malicious compliance' was coined to describe those unhappy 'jobsworth' staff who do only the bare minimum as a protest against their employer. This is the problem of measurement by proxy. It is a type of misdirection, whether it is used for a good or a bad end. And it is true that where a thing is too complex to be measured accurately, indicators become a convenient code for underlying behaviour. What has happened in the case of share price is that it has become a measurement in itself, rather than just one indicator among many. Of course, sophisticated analysts know this, but trading algorithms are only as sophisticated as the indicators used in their programming. While news feeds are now being formatted to be read by them, it will be some time before they can mimic the processing complexity of the human brain, particularly when it comes to deciding something as unscientific as the health - and the future – of a company, let alone the reliability of a source.

The share price directly feeds into the other key metric involved: return on equity (ROE). This is one of the ratios commonly used in finance, valuation, and accounting as a quick way to analyse company results so that they can be compared easily with previous performance or the performance of industry peers. Other popular measurements are ratios like earnings per share (EPS), return on capital employed (ROCE), or earnings before interest, taxes, depreciation and amortization (EBITDA). Because ROE is a measurement of net income after tax, divided by shareholder equity, it is extremely susceptible to financial engineering. In the market's heyday, many an MBA student was taught that 'debt was cheaper than equity', where equity is about raising money through shares, and debt is about raising money through loans. Debt interest costs tend to be tax-deductible, unlike the cost of equity financing, and dividends often 'cost' more than paying bank interest. A loan has the capacity to increase ROE by boosting the top line of the equation, while fresh equity would dilute it by increasing the bottom line of the equation. Ironically, the ROE metric only covers a small amount of the balance sheet, because equity financing is such a tiny proportion of most organizations' asset base, but it is easy to measure - and easy to manipulate - making it ideal for institutional investors to whom agency theory has handed this suspiciously blank cheque.

One example of ROE manipulation is the popular practice of buying back company shares, which boosts ROE even further by effectively reducing the number of shares in the equation.

Using US data as an example, in 2011, 354 of the Standard & Poor's 500 companies spent $333 billion on share buy-backs, more than they spent on dividends. Looking longitudinally, the econometrician Alok Bhargava's analysis of 2,000 US industrial firms shows that about a quarter were conducting buy-backs in 1992. A peak of 50 per cent was reached in 1998, and levels returned to around 40 per cent in 2006. While this practice is often justified as a useful way to 'tidy up' shareholder liability, or a responsible use of excess cash, it is most often used to manage the share price and boost ROE, and is now widespread. One particularly unfortunate side-effect of the practice was that many of the banks who indulged in it found they had spent all of their spare cash just as the credit crunch hit. So, in November 2007, the $7.5 billion equity investment that Citigroup secured from the Abu Dhabi Investment Authority was almost as much as it had spent on buy-backs in 2006 and 2007; Merrill Lynch spent more than $14 billion in repurchases in 2006–7, but by January 2008 had given up a 12.7 per cent equity stake to raise $9 billion from foreign investors; and Morgan Stanley, which spent $7 billion in buy-backs in 2006–7, had to trade a 9.9 per cent equity stake with China's sovereign wealth fund for $5 billion.

However, the assumption of shareholder supremacy is not only toxic, it is intuitively wrong. The function of shares is to provide occasional capital to a given business. For many businesses, this only happens a few times over the life of the corporation: once at launch, and maybe two or three times later on to finance milestone investments or acquisitions. Indeed, shares act as a special type of loan financing, except that shareholders may lose their investment as well as reap a profit, hence their use in Shariah-compliant banking to share risk and reward and avoid involvement with usury. Indeed, it is precisely because of the shadow cast by usury laws in general that joint stock companies – whereby two or more individuals invest by paying for a 'share' in the enterprise – became the most popular form of business organization in the first place. Historically, sharing risk and reward through some kind of partnership was the only legal way to raise capital.

But an analysis of modern shareholding shows how bizarre the obsession with shareholder value now is. Looking at data produced by the UK Office for National Statistics based on shares quoted on the London Stock Exchange, around 40 per cent of UK shares are currently held by foreign investors. No breakdown of this 40 per cent is available, but the remaining 60 per cent shareholding can be apportioned in the following way: individuals own a sixth of it, and institutions five-sixths. So we can immediately dispense with the caricature of the shareholder as a loyal, tweed-suited old man who stumped up his hard-earned cash to prop up the business when it needed him, and who can therefore not be left out in the cold in his dotage. The vast majority of an organization's 'shareholders' are probably hunched in front of a spreadsheet, monitoring share prices for their customers, and switching stocks if movements threaten the integrity of the portfolio as a whole. This picture is brought into sharp relief by modern trading practices. Ignoring for the time being distortions created by the secondary markets, equity trading is now so sophisticated that in many cases it is executed automatically by computer, using algorithms designed to take advantage of infinitesimal changes in price (and split-second early warning of them) to keep a portfolio within given parameters. This 'high-frequency trading' has been taking place at least since the US Securities and Exchange Commission (SEC) authorized electronic exchanges in the United States in 1998, presumably on the grounds that this hyper-liquidity could only assist the price mechanism in a trading environment. Now, there is a race to speed up this already superfast technology, with the new Illinois–New Jersey data link utilizing microwaves to achieve transactions that are almost instantaneous. Just to indicate the scale of this activity, in 2010 the *Wall Street Journal* reported that high-frequency trading comprised 53 per cent of stockmarket trading volume, although estimates for some exchanges take this figure up to 80 per cent. And the speed? According to Michael Lewis, it takes a human eye at least 100 milliseconds to blink, but it takes less than a tenth of this time for a trade to travel between Chicago and New York.

This activity can have a dramatic effect. As a specific example of this, consider the research carried out by the physics department of the University of Miami into so-called 'flash crashes', like the mysterious one that occurred on 6 May 2010. That afternoon, the Dow Jones Industrial Average suddenly plunged 1,000 points - about 9 per cent - only to recover within minutes once an automatic stabilizer on the futures exchange cut in and paused trading. It was the second largest ever swing, and the biggest one-day decline in the history of the Index. The Miami research looked at transactions on multiple stocks across multiple exchanges between 2006–11, looking particularly at those transactions that occurred in sub-second time frames and were thus driven by algorithm. The research uncovered 18,520 ultra-fast anomalies in stock-price activity, either crashes or spikes, where 'ultra-fast' means those transactions occurring beneath the sub-650 millisecond threshold for crashes and the sub-950 millisecond threshold for spikes. This revealed an average of one momentary spike or crash per trading day. It's still not clear why these happen, but the fact that the algorithms are now programmed to respond to news headlines is likely to lead to more chaos. On 23 April 2013, a tweet on The Associated Press' Twitter feed indicated that two explosions had occurred in the White House, injuring President Barack Obama. While it took only minutes for the tweet to be exposed as a hoax, it was too late. The Dow had already plunged more than 140 points, and bond yields fell. Reuters estimated that the temporary loss of market cap in the S&P 500 alone was $136.5 billion. While some of this activity was dealer-led, the scale and intensity of the spike was driven by high-frequency trading, which had taken the tweet at face value.

High-frequency trading on equities exchanges is actually in decline, as the 'bots' move away from equities into currency trading and futures in search of better returns. While the potential for this type of activity to crash organizations through the equity markets is alarming enough, the spectre of it crashing a nation through currency trading is deeply worrying. But whether or not algorithmic trading is destabilizing, morally questionable or potentially useful, the Miami research serves to illustrate how radically different today's 'shareholder' world has become. Sources vary on the average time for which a share is now held. Some say 11 seconds, some say 22, some claim an average between 20 and 30 seconds. Even if high-frequency trading on equities exchanges reduces, perhaps through taxation, the fact that a consensus would agree an average holding time of under a minute means that the immediate problem facing a company obsessed with shareholder value is, which shareholder, and when? Who exactly is the company accountable to, given this blur of faces in any given day, let alone the army of shareholders fading in and out over an entire reporting year? Even looking just at bank stocks, the Bank of England's Andrew Haldane reports that average holding periods for shares in US and UK banks had fallen from around three years in 1998 to around three months by 2008. And apart from the blink-and-you-miss-them shareholders, what does it mean to be dealing with layers of intermediaries between the shares themselves and their beneficial owners, given the explosion of investment consultants, asset managers, trustees, 'funds of funds' and others who now sit between an owner and an asset? Can a company truly tell what their shareholders want, without asking them directly (and frequently), given modern patterns in shareholding?

But, as a strategy to return profits to investors, it is true that 'shareholder value' appears to have worked, at least in the short term. Data produced for the US Congress on US corporations shows a shift between 1960 and 2000 from a 40 per cent ratio of dividend paid out of after-tax profits to a 50 per cent payout ratio from 1980 onwards. So those shareholders who wanted more yield will not have been disappointed, in that they have generally been receiving a higher level of profit as dividend. And we have already noted the 'efficiency' argument about freeing up lazy capital to be redeployed through redistribution elsewhere in the economy.

But this is not the full story. In his discussion on 'downsize and redistribute', Lazonick contrasts employment in the top fifty largest US industrial corporations between 1969 and 1991, showing a drop in employment from 6.4 million people (7.5 per cent of the civilian labour force) to 5.2 million people (4.2 per cent of the labour force), while the payout ratio of dividends to after-tax profits increased from 37.2 per cent in 1966 to a high of 53 per cent in 1974, averaging 42.3 per cent throughout the 1970s and 50 per cent in the 1980s and thereafter. These numbers indicate a deeper reality, that during the era of 'downsize and distribute' income inequality has accelerated, driven down at the bottom end by the downward pressure on wages and employment, and driven up at the top end by increased return on equity. US figures suggest that 80 per cent of households own less than 2 per cent of share capital, with the top 1 per cent owning around 37 per cent of all outstanding corporate equities, and figures for the rest of the world appear to be comparable. Wilkinson and Pickett's book *The Spirit Level* expounds the inequality thesis in some detail, with Thomas Piketty's book *Capital in the Twenty-First Century* explaining the multiplier effect of inherited wealth. Broadly, the steeper the social gradient of any given societal problem, the more strongly it is related to income inequality, so any society that exhibits this accelerating gap between rich and poor will be storing up serious problems for the future. Data for the US and the UK shows that the gap between the richest and poorest 10 per cent has increased by 40 per cent since the mid-1970s, which maps to a parallel increase in a range of social problems. In the UK alone, Oxfam reports that the five richest families are wealthier than the bottom 20 per cent of the population. This means that just five households are worth more than 12.6 million people combined, which just happens to be about the same as the number of people living below the poverty line in the UK. Piketty's research shows that this gap tends to accelerate from generation to generation because of the 'halo' effect of inherited wealth, which, through their superior ability to invest, exponentially increases the rich's share over time.

Apart from the switch of resource away from longer-term investment towards short-term reward, another cost of the apparent success of the shareholder value regime has been the disproportionate rise in senior executive pay. An analysis of the major US corporations between 1980–95 shows that, while profits in the time period did increase by 145 per cent, CEO pay over the same fifteen-year period increased by almost 500 per cent. While this would seem to support defenders of agency theory, the prosaic truth is likely to be that the largely institutional shareholders involved have been more than happy to approve increases in remuneration for their fellow professionals, given the gains their shareholdings have made, and the general uplift in salaries and bonuses that many of them are themselves enjoying as members of the financial services community. This rise in executive pay has been at the relative and absolute cost of those lower down the payscale. Again, the research reported in *The Spirit Level* provides ample evidence that accelerating differences in income inequality will ultimately stoke the fires of societal breakdown. While the ratio between top and bottom pay in organizations has widened, as we have already seen, 'downsize and distribute' has also been about taking cost out of the business, often using technology, outsourcing and offshoring to reduce headcount. This strategy of living off the past by not investing in the future does boost short-term gain, as does any form of asset-stripping. But it does pose a challenge to those responsible for corporate governance in deciding to prioritize the present so aggressively over the future.

Apart from the problem of 'who' the shareholder really is, and whether shareholder value works as a strategy over the longer term, there is a legal problem with the assumption that it is the shareholders who own the business. Even if one could theoretically isolate each shareholder and run the business collectively but in each of their particular interests, a closer look shows that this concept is actually another toxic assumption. Let's have a look at what shareholders actually 'own'. In a UK public limited company, the ownership of a share conveys a right to a share certificate, the right to ask the court to call a general meeting, the right to vote, the right to a dividend if one is paid, and the right to have the company wound up. Other rights include the right to an AGM and access to various notices, registers and annual accounts. And a shareholding can of course be sold. But what does 'ownership' then mean in this context? If I own a house, I can do what I like with it, within the law. But owning a 'share' is not really owning a company in the same way. If a company goes bad, I lose my stake and all of the rights listed above, but am protected against other losses through limited liability. If it goes well, I get a stream of dividends. If it goes so well that the company gets sold on or cashed in in some other way, I get a share of the spoils, in the same way that if I sold my house I would reap the profit. But I don't 'own' the company, I just receive certain rights along with my share certificate, none of which really give me much say in the day-to-day running of the entity, or any claim on profits unless the board declares a dividend. To use our house metaphor, as a shareholder I am much more like a member of the local neighbourhood watch than I am the 'owner' of the house, for all the practical control I really have over the big decisions affecting my property, yet I stand to benefit or lose out from its fate. As we saw from the argument of the principal–agent problem, the rhetoric of shareholder as owner is both compelling and widely assumed, and it has been immortalized by negative language from the likes of Marx about capitalists exploiting the proletariat through their ownership of the means of production. But, like the 'invisible hand', the idea of shareholder as owner evaporates under close scrutiny. As Paul Davies, the former Allen & Overy Professor in Corporate Law at Oxford says, 'I'm not sure any self-respecting academic today believes shareholders own the company'.

It may sound like splitting hairs to labour this distinction between owning shares and owning the company, but it is a key point. It was the Americans Adolf Berle, a lawyer, and Gardiner Means, an economist, who most famously argued that the effective separation of ownership and control that this implies is a problem for corporations. Way back in 1932, their seminal *The Modern Corporation and Private Property* identified the issue of the shortfalls of competence and responsibility involved, which has set the governance agenda ever since. Jensen and Meckling reference Berle and Means in their landmark paper on agency theory, but this and shareholder value are just the latest in a series of remedies proposed over the intervening years. Indeed, the legal distinction between ownership and control was made far earlier on.

Paddy Ireland at the University of Kent notes that the landmark English case of *Bligh v. Brent* (1837) established that shareholders had no direct interest, legal or equitable, in the property owned by the company, just a right to dividends and a right to assign their shares for value. By 1860, the shares of joint stock companies had been established as legal objects in their own right. This separation of them, as forms of property independent of the assets of the company, effectively disassociated them from the assets of the company. These assets were now owned exclusively by the company, while the share capital of the company was the sole property of the shareholder. Ireland argues that this rather thin idea of ownership without control was deliberate. This is because the legal vehicle of the 'company' was primarily a gambit to share financial risk and reward without falling foul of the usury prohibition, which otherwise effectively prevented enterprise by starving it of loan capital. Most investors by this point had a range of financial interests, and might well have preferred the loan route had it been available to them. So, in the main, they tended only to be interested in the enterprise itself insofar as they were liable for it, a residual interest which evaporated with the advent of ubiquitous limited liability.

As an aside, the history of American 'anti-trust' law, or law designed to prevent monopoly, also casts light on this historical parting of the ways. In the 1880s, Standard Oil's solicitors suggested that the resurrection of the legal 'trust' vehicle would be the best way to amalgamate the forty state-based companies that formed the Standard Oil alliance in order to achieve the economies of scale that could be gained from centralized control. This was effected by the shareholders of the forty companies giving their voting shares to a central trust company in return for tradable trust certificates that carried the right to receive income but not to vote. This effectively created the first 'holding company', emphasizing the idea that a shareholder's only concern is financial. The explosion in these trusts, as states vied with each other to be an attractive legal host, led to the 1890 Sherman Act, the first federal competition statute, and the term 'anti-trust' as a synonym for competition law entered the lexicon. In the US, this thinking was upheld in a landmark case in 1916, long before the academics got involved, in which the Michigan Supreme Court ruled that 'a business corporation is organized and carried on primarily for the profit of the shareholders'.

Current criticism of 'shareholder value' assumes that shareholders who seem more interested in financial return than in the business in which they are invested is a peculiarly modern phenomenon. History suggests that this may have been the case for far longer than has been popularly supposed, however, and that the issue is more a toxic fault line in corporate law than a temporary fashion. Indeed, the categories of 'rentier' and 'capitalist' were included in the UK national census until the 1960s, as options under the rather judgemental category of 'no gainful occupation stated'. True, the rise of the institutional investor, the relaxation in regulation and advances in technology have elevated share-trading to a highly sophisticated art, but this background shows that the rot had already set in well before these changes accelerated the process of alienation.

What alternatives might there be? Haldane suggests a simple switch from return on equity to return on assets, because the latter measure covers the whole balance sheet. And, because it is not 'flattered by leverage' it can do a better job of adjusting for risk. Under an ROE regime, the shareholders, who may only have an interest in around 5 per cent of the balance sheet, have undue influence over the rest of the asset base, and are incentivized to risk it in its entirety by colluding with equity-holding company directors to boost short-term returns. Moreover, he suggests that using ROA would have had a better historical effect on executive pay. Using his world of banking as an example, if a bank CEO's pay had been indexed to ROE in 1990, by 2007 CEO compensation would have reached $26 million, which matches actual payouts. But if you recalculate this for, say, the CEOs of the seven largest US banks, using ROA from 1989, by 2007 their compensation would have risen from $2.8 million to 'just' $3.4 million. As a comparison, this would replace an ROE-based rise to 500 times median US household income with an ROA-based rise to 68 times median US household income. But this does not really go far enough, given that skewed measurement is more of a symptom than an underlying cause of the problem. In any case, a 2008 report by the International Labour Organization concluded that there was little or no empirical evidence of a relationship between executive pay and company performance, suggesting that excessive salaries are more to do with the dominant bargaining position of executives than anything else.

Given the fundamental problem of divorce between shareholders and companies, something more drastic is required. Issues of ownership in particular will be revisited in the context of discussion of our final toxic assumption: limited liability as the prevailing model for business. The matter of wider accountability, however, has already found expression in the 'stakeholder' agenda, which offers a rich seam for prospecting. What started as 'corporate social responsibility' or 'triple bottom line accounting' has matured into a realization that taking the wider view is a core board responsibility, as part of its strategic and fiduciary role. In many jurisdictions this is now enshrined not only in company law but in the accompanying regulatory, governance and reporting codes of conduct. Since 2000, the United Nations Global Compact has led the way in persuading companies internationally, whether or not their jurisdiction demands it in law, to align their operations and strategies with a set of ten principles concerning human rights, labour, environment and anti-corruption, and to take action in support of UN objectives like the Millennium Development Goals, and the Sustainable Development Goals due to replace these in 2015. It is the largest corporate responsibility initiative in the world, with over 9,000 signatories, based in 140 countries. Apart from these kinds of initiatives, many companies are finding ways to recognize more explicitly the interests of employees, pensioners, customers, partners, suppliers, regulators and local communities, as well as the shareholders themselves. In the days of 'hyper-transparency' this is simply good business practice, particularly when consumer brands are so vulnerable to bad press. Indeed, Germany's two-tier board system has always facilitated the inclusion on the supervisory board of interest groups like banks, local politicians, business partners and trade unions, as well as significant shareholders. Elsewhere, whether it takes the form of advisory boards, board observers, regular consultations or reciprocal secondments, only the most myopic companies are ignoring this new reality. But more could be done, as too often the department that deals with stakeholder concerns reports into marketing, rather than strategy or the board direct, which tends to betray a rather cynical motivation and prevents such practices becoming mainstream.

In fact, charity practice is instructive in this regard. The Charity Commission for England and Wales expresses it thus. Trustees have ultimate responsibility for delivering 'charitable outcomes for the benefit of the public for which it has been set up' and for remaining 'true to the charitable purpose and objects set out in its governing document'. This is an interesting spin on the parallel responsibilities of a company director, because it particularly references the founding document. While directors are also required to act in accordance with their company's constitution, this is not so culturally central, and tends to cede in practice to more immediate concerns. This is particularly relevant where a company has been through a series of transformations, and so may no longer be in the same business in which it started (e.g., Nokia, which over its 150-year history has morphed from being a paper mill, a manufacturer of rubber boots and car tyres, a generator of electricity and a TV manufacturer, to becoming a global telecommunications company). But hanging on to what Will Hutton has called the core organizational 'reason to be' can act as a useful earthing device. He often talks about Unilever's founding purpose which, when it was founded in the 1880s, was 'to build the best everyday things for everyday folk' and the spirit of this mission is still alive in the Unilever corporate culture. Jim Collins and Jerry Porras famously made this point in their 1994 management classic *Built to Last*, which included in its formula 'more than profits', which was about companies who sustained success over the long term being true to their core purpose, e.g., Merck's 'preserving and improving human life' or Disney's 'use our imagination to bring happiness to millions'. While it is in vogue for companies to develop straplines, these tend to be rather empty branding exercises and rarely encapsulate the spirit of the enterprise. Connecting with the highest purpose of the company, however, taps into something of its founding zeitgeist, and acts as a useful corrective to a narrow focus on shareholder value.

The toxic assumption of the absolute sovereignty of the shareholder, then, no longer makes any sense. Given their legal status, and the fact that modern patterns of shareholding makes them an increasingly elusive species, an appeal to the shareholder now resembles more of a veiled appeal to the self-interest of the stock-incentivized senior management, or an appeal to the corporate equivalent of Santa Claus in an attempt to get the children to behave. This distracting assumption has driven unhealthy short-termism, inculcated bad habits concerning measurement and strategy, and encouraged companies to adopt too narrow a definition of their responsibilities. While many of these problems are already being corrected by useful pressure from the sustainability and corporate social responsibility agendas, companies need to be more proactive about putting their shareholders back into perspective. A useful starting point would be to review their relative importance compared with other stakeholders, many of whom add significant current value to the business, rather than having an often rather distant and minor historical claim.

Chapter 7

The assumption of the legitimacy of the limited liability model

According to the theologian Michael Black, the invention of 'the corporation' owes its existence to the Franciscan monks, who needed a legal device to allow them to hold monastic property without breaking their vow of poverty. In 1246, to solve the problem for them, Pope Innocent IV issued a papal judgement using the term *persona ficta,* a fictitious person, to characterize the entirety of a collective group, and the idea of the modern corporation was born. From the outset, he established the convention of a board of 'procurators' to administer the new entity as an independent construct, and upheld this independence in subsequent papal rulings and judgements. In England in 1461, this new device allowed the newly enthroned King Edward IV to get his hands on Henry VI's privately owned Duchy of Lancaster by establishing it as a separate legal entity, installing himself as director and stripping it of its assets.

The words 'company' and 'corporation' tend to be used interchangeably, although the former is perhaps more a UK term while the US favours the latter. Interestingly, while 'corporation' derives from the Latin word for body, 'company' derives from the Latin words for sharing bread, which is perhaps why the term company is used to refer to partnerships as well as to corporations per se. The UK's oldest company, according to John Micklethwait and Adrian Wooldridge, is the Aberdeen Harbour Board, set up by charter in 1136; the US's oldest company is Harvard University, chartered in 1636. The oldest surviving multinational is Canada's Hudson's Bay Company, originally founded in 1670 to sell furs, and now selling a range of retail products through subsidiaries such as the US department store Lord & Taylor.

In the UK, the history of the company really starts with the common practice of sending ships abroad on trading missions. Often with monopoly protection from the crown, these would travel the seas in search of silks and spices, new trading partners and new lands to conquer. Latterly, these voyages increasingly specialized in the slave trade. Often merchants or private individuals would create a one-off partnership or company to finance a single voyage or fleet, anxiously awaiting news of its return in one of London's famous coffee houses. This is the origin of the phrase 'when my ship comes in' and became formalized in the Underwriting Room at Lloyd's by the famous Lutine Bell. The bell was traditionally struck once for the loss of a ship and twice for her return, and was still in use as late as 1989.

Over the years, the company as a legal device has become increasingly sophisticated, developing a legal persona to the extent that it has become popularly anthropomorphized by the critics, most famously so by Joel Bakan. His book – and successful film – was called *The Corporation: The Pathological Pursuit of Profit and Power*. In it, he gets Dr Robert Hare, author of the famous psychopathy scale, to apply it to the corporation as an entity, finding a spookily exact match. Indeed, corporate personality has developed to the extent that in many countries, companies can now be prosecuted for corporate manslaughter.

While in the UK this has been possible since 1965, only one successful prosecution had ever been made. Following the 1993 Lyme Bay canoeing tragedy, in which four teenagers died, Peter Kite, the owner of OLL Limited, was jailed for three years and his company fined £60,000. After many controversial cases had failed under existing legislation, new legislation was introduced in 2007 – the Corporate Manslaughter and Corporate Homicide Act – with a suggested penalty of 5–10 per cent of annual company turnover. On 17 February 2011, Cotswold Geotechnical became the first – and to date only – company to be prosecuted under the new legislation, being fined £385,000 for the death of a geologist after the collapse of a trial pit in Gloucestershire.

While a detailed history of the company need not delay us here, it is important to track the emergence of limited liability within this larger story. First, limited liability used to be rare, and the presumption was always that parties in a business partnership or corporation were liable for losses as well as for gains. In English law, exceptions were made in the fifteenth century for monastic communities and for trade guilds that held property in common. There was little support for the use of the concept of limited liability more widely, because of the moral hazard it represented, and limited liability had to be granted by charter or by Act of Parliament. In an environment where usury laws still held (they were not repealed in the UK until 1854), joint-stock companies were the most attractive way to finance enterprise, as they allowed investors to pool resources in exchange for a proportional 'share' in the expected profits. However, the riskier the enterprise, the harder it was to get investors involved. When these involved huge projects for public goods like canals or railways, the government had an interest in incentivizing investors to take part, and the business of granting dedicated charters or promulgating special Acts of Parliament became increasingly cumbersome. The French had also stolen a march by creating a far simpler legal process in 1807 and, according to Micklethwait and Wooldridge, by the 1850s some twenty English firms had set themselves up in France to take advantage of this device. So, in 1855, the Limited Liability Act was passed in England, which permitted limited liability to any company with more than twenty-five shareholders (excepting the insurance companies, who had to wait until the Companies Act of 1862). Subsequent Acts eroded this numerical requirement, from twenty-five to seven shareholders in the 1856 Joint Stock Companies Act, down to one today.

The Christian Socialists were reportedly keen on limited liability, because they thought that it would democratize shareholding, enrich the poor and reduce class conflict. But this acceptance of limited liability as normal for business was not universally seen as a positive move. The Rice and Lloyd Webber of their day, Gilbert and Sullivan, wrote a satirical musical called *Utopia, Limited* as a reaction to the Joint Stock Company Act of 1862. It contained these lines:

> If you succeed, your profits are stupendous. And if you fail, pop goes your eighteen-pence. Make the money-spinner spin! For you only stand to win.

This central issue, that investors would now only stand to lose their original stake, has been widely credited with accelerating the boom in enterprise since. It has also created a variety of problems for the market, the chief of which is a moral problem, in that it seems rather unjust for there no longer to be any downside for shareholders, despite much rhetoric to the contrary about shareholders taking 'all the risk'. But this problem has bred further, more subtle, problems concerning risk appetite, which are compounded in the light of the previous discussion on agency theory and shareholder value.

Of these problems, risk appetite is the most serious, because it is worsened by the co-ownership of shares across the governance divide. The so-called 'limited liability effect' means that shareholders care more about gains than about losses, because they are risking only their share capital. This incentivizes them to encourage aggressive growth strategies, supported by incentive packages designed to maximize their return. This means that both shareholders and stock-incentivized senior management are united in a focus on share price maximization, with all the dangers we have seen that this can bring. In particular, modern patterns of both shareholding and trading make a short-term get-rich-quick strategy the only one that now makes any investment sense.

The nature of the precise drivers of risk, and the effect of differing combinations of debt and equity financing, has been a popular discussion in academic circles. Recent debate tends to side more with equity (raising money through shares) than with debt (raising money through loans), in spite of the current fashion for firms to behave to the contrary. For instance, a 1989 model created by the Canadian economists Brander and Spencer suggested that equity keeps a firm more 'honest' than debt, because of the 'effort effect of equity'. This effect holds that equity keeps a company on the straight and narrow because an accountability to shareholders feels weightier than accountability to a bank. Further, the 1999 model created by the LSE economist Faure-Grimaud shows that debt causes firms to compete less aggressively than equity. This is because taking a risk that does not pay off with debt causes a company to default on its loans, whereas taking risks with shareholder money, in the context of limited liability, does not risk their capital, and it is human nature to be more motivated to avoid downsides than to prefer upsides. This, coupled with the limited liability effect, unites the shareholders and the company in a commitment to growth (at least in the short term). So, Faure-Grimaud would argue strongly for a model whereby ownership is shared through stock-holding, ideally with limited liability, to prevent company indolence and lassitude. While these findings must be heavily caveated, as they assume agency theory, shareholder value and the predictive ability of models, they show just how strongly the spectre of shareholder reaction features in the corporate imagination. The shareholder looms larger, and in quite a different way than the spectre of a disappointed debtor, even though it is the debtor that has the prior claim to a firm's assets. As we have seen, this is rather ironic, given that the implied influence of shareholders is largely illusory. Not only are shareholders restricted to voting at an AGM and very little else, but modern patterns of shareholding make their engagement with the business rather a nonsense. But as we have also seen, it is in the interests of a share-incentivized executive to talk up the spectre of the shareholder to encourage a focus on share price that will boost their own remuneration.

Another downside of the ease with which the limited liability model segues into a corporate strategy based on shareholder value is the resultant tunnel vision that blanks out the wider stakeholder community. As we have seen in the discussions on pricing and shareholder value, the UN and others have worked hard to get a company's 'embeddedness' recognized, leading to changes in law and governance in many jurisdictions to admit the legitimate interests of stakeholders. It is as if the word 'limited' has eclipsed the word 'company', which is more about the human collective actively engaged in the enterprise than about its historical funding. Perhaps it is overly whimsical in this context but in discussing the Franciscan roots of the company format, Michael Black is at pains to recall its heritage as a relational concept, albeit one that was informed by specifically Christian notions about the Trinity, and the Church as the body of Christ. Its 'ethical ecology' is one that emphasizes community and mutual submission, which chimes with my themes of co-operation and externalities, as organizations interact and intra-act to create the products and services they sell. Because the ultimate effect of limiting liability seems to have been to create fractures rather than to heal them, this sort of thinking is perhaps more relevant than it might at first appear.

While the limited liability model has become the pre-eminent form of business collective, as a device it is primarily about structuring finance in a way that stimulates the emergence of enterprise to drive economic growth. As we have seen, this device owes a lot to the historical and cultural context from which it emerged. It was Ronald Coase who famously told a group of Dundee students in 1932 that the only logical reason for a company's existence is to minimize transaction costs through the economies of scale offered by some kind of collective endeavour. So what other models of collective endeavour are there, and how do they compare in terms of risk profile and sustainable economic performance?

In 2010, Will Hutton chaired the Ownership Commission, which was instigated by the UK government. Its remit was to conduct a comprehensive analysis of business ownership in Britain in order to examine the extent to which it was supporting or inhibiting successful, long-term value creation by business in all its various forms. Its findings do not cover the public and charity sectors, although some of the business formats discussed have a degree of crossover into these terrains. The Commission's work involved an assessment of the governance and ownership of both the limited company format and of non-limited company forms, including family ownership, mutuals, co-operatives and employee-owned enterprises. It reported in March 2012, with a key conclusion about the risk that the current 'PLC mono-culture' presents to economic resilience: the Commission found that around half of Britain's GDP is currently delivered by limited companies, a vastly skewed proportion when compared to other countries. Its report argued that a more diversified corporate sector would result in greater stability, more accountability to consumers, reduced systemic risk and more competition. Its case rests not only on arguments from ecology and evolutionary biology but also on the 'herding effect' that is created by a monopolizing business model, which can lead to dangerous homogeneity and groupthink. This approach can also become self-perpetuating, as professional services firms increasingly specialize in the prevailing models and have no incentive to support alternatives.

The report usefully contrasts the limited liability model with several other business models, which vary widely in their purpose. On the one hand, there are those businesses that are unashamedly in it for the money. On the other, there are those whose aim is the business activity itself. In between are a range of hybrids. At one end of the spectrum, private equity tends to epitomize an extreme form of the 'shareholder value' strategy. A private equity fund gathers money from its partners - who may be private individuals or institutions - together with loans from financial institutions, and uses them to buy up under-performing companies. These they streamline, perhaps by reducing the workforce or selling assets, with a view to increasing their value for a fast sale. By definition, the owners are only interested in exiting at a profit, either by a trade sale or by stock market flotation. They therefore tend to guard their investment closely, and will often intervene to select key management personnel or dictate strategy if they feel their investment is at risk. Private equity ownership is reckoned to account for less than 1 per cent of UK companies. At the other end of the spectrum, state-run enterprises tend to be retained in a form of public ownership because of fears that an untrammelled profit motive would damage the service on offer. In practice these vary widely, although the principle is still to provide some form of democratic control over these retained services through the political process. While public policy on ownership ebbs and flows, many countries reserve services like justice, defence, education, health and utilities to the state, some of which are run like charities (on a not-for-profit basis), and some of which are run like businesses (for profit). For example, the world's largest telecoms company, China Mobile, is state-run, and state-owned energy firms like Russia's Gazprom and Saudi Aramco account for over three-quarters of the world's oil production. In the UK, there are state hybrids too, where the government has a majority or substantial shareholding, like Royal Mail, Channel 4 or Eurostar, and these are run at arm's length by the Shareholder Executive. In November 2008, the UK government also created a company - with the Treasury as sole shareholder - called 'UK

Financial Investments' to manage the state's shareholdings in the range of banks, like RBS, that had been partially or wholly 'rescued' in the wake of the credit crunch.

Sovereign wealth funds bridge the gap between the two extremes of private equity and state-ownership. These are state-owned investment funds which might comprise state savings, pension investments, oil funds or other financial holdings. For example, Norway's Government Pension Fund, the largest pension fund in the world, was created to hold all of the surplus wealth produced by the country's petroleum income. Sovereign wealth funds are used primarily to generate financial return, but may also be used diplomatically or defensively to buy into useful sectors abroad. Currently, the Chinese government is buying into African and South American commodities, while some of the Middle Eastern sovereign wealth funds have been persuaded by distressed Western banks to take significant positions in them to guarantee their future, often as an alternative to host-state bailout.

The other business models that range across this spectrum are family-owned businesses, partnerships, co-operatives, mutuals and employee-owned firms. Family-owned businesses and partnerships tend to combine ownership with control, in that the owners are most often also the senior management of the business. This is not always the case, particularly as family-owned businesses mature and many families exercise their ownership through a residual position on the board instead of a hands-on executive role. Neither is it unknown for there to be 'silent' partners in a partnership. But in the main, partnerships such as the large legal and accounting firms, and the majority of family-owned enterprises, unite these two ownership and control roles, solving at one stroke any residual 'agency' problem there might be. Hutton reports that family ownership accounts for around 60 per cent of European businesses, including 25 per cent of the continent's top 100 businesses. In the UK, around 10 per cent of firms are family-owned, contributing about 30 per cent of UK GDP. The latest UK data suggests similar percentages for partnerships, and it is now possible to form a limited liability partnership, with its attendant risks and benefits. Partnerships remain attractive as a vehicle because profits are shared between the partners, who generally constitute a smaller group of people than would be the case in distributing dividends among shareholders in a traditional limited company.

Of the final three illustrative business models - co-operatives, mutuals and employee-owned firms - co-operatives and mutuals are similar in that their customers own the business. Often they have been created by a group of people who cannot on their own gain access to the services they need, but collectively they can achieve scale and credibility. This model is used by credit unions and many of the traditional building societies, as well as those farming co-operatives across the world who combine to establish a competitive wholesale or retail presence. Mutuals and co-operatives are owned by their members, each of whom has an equal vote. The members elect the board, and surpluses tend to be ploughed back into the business. While interest is sometimes payable, the focus of this type of business model is on providing goods and services to people on a fair basis. In the UK, mutuals represent about 5 per cent of economic activity, providing 3.5 per cent of total employment. The UK's co-operative retail trade has about 8 per cent market share, with Co-operative Food being the

UK's fifth largest food retailer. The Co-operative Group as a whole is the UK's largest mutual business, owned by over six million consumers. As well as its retail presence, it runs financial services, owning 20 per cent of the Co-operative Banking Group. It is also the UK's largest funeral services provider, and runs Britain's largest farming operation. The Group operates 4,800 retail trading outlets, employs more than 106,000 people and has an annual turnover of more than £13 billion. The world's largest worker co-operative is Mondragón in Spain, which was founded in 1956 and has interests in finance, industry, retail and education, and is the seventh largest Spanish company by turnover.

While mutuals and consumer co-operatives give customers ownership, the business model *du jour* is employee ownership (sometimes called a worker co-operative). This model solves any problem arising from a separation of ownership and control by giving all employees a stake in the business. The poster-child for this format in the UK is the John Lewis Partnership, a department store and grocery chain, formed in 1920. The employee-ownership format differs from the modern limited company strategy of granting senior management shares, as its integrity as a business model depends on democratic ownership from top to bottom, such that every worker with over a year's service has a stake in the enterprise, which is majority-owned by the employee body. While an employee-ownership structure can be used from the start, it is more common for privately owned or publicly quoted companies to transition into employee ownership by being bought by the employees, either directly or in phases. Because the vast majority of the employees in this sort of employee buy-out will not be on the kind of salaries that would give them access to this level of capital, they borrow money for a leveraged buyout. This normally passes ownership of the company into a trust for the employees, paid for by the company itself over time, which assists with stability and the company's ability to attract funding. The trust device also means that the shares can be vested in the trust to create an internal market, both for the repurchase of shares from staff who are retiring or leaving, and their reallocation to new hires.

Looking at these models, ownership however defined is variously vested in the providers of capital, the employees (senior management or more generally) or customers, with the state being a special case of this latter category. Logically, there should also be a model whereby suppliers also own the business, which would be the rationale behind the diamond and oil cartels, and incidences of 'vertical integration' where companies extend over the supply chain to control more of the journey from raw material to customer. Examples of this type would be everything from Oxford University's Isis Innovation, a wholly owned subsidiary set up to commercialize the university's intellectual property, to farm co-operatives and local farmers' markets. However they are constituted, each of these models differs not only in legal and financial form, but also in the types of governance challenges they face, and their risk appetite. The Ownership Commission is at particular pains to point out that a business ecology that embraced a diversity of these models would be more resilient to economic shocks, and would give all parties more choice about return on investment – financial and otherwise.

In the UK, there are two new models that have recently been devised, both of which offer interesting scope for further innovation. The first of these was created for a particular sector, the UK National Health Service. A vehicle called an NHS foundation trust was established through the Health and Social Care (Community Health and Standards) Act 2003, which was consolidated into the National Health Service Act 2006. This was a new type of company, a 'public benefit corporation' specific to the NHS, authorized and regulated by an independent regulator. The trusts are accountable to their local communities through a system of local ownership. They can borrow money within limits set by the regulator, retain surpluses and decide on service development for their local populations. While they are required to lay their annual reports and accounts before Parliament each year, they are free from central government control and strategic health authority performance management. The second of these new models, the 'Community Interest Company' (CIC), was established under the Companies (Audit, Investigations and Community Enterprise) Act 2004. While there is no single legal model for this new form, it is designed for social enterprises that want an 'asset lock' to permit their profits to be used for the public good, so that any surplus produced is reinvested in the business or the community. The format is regulated, but more lightly than is a charity. The social entrepreneurs involved can serve as paid members of the CIC board, and a CIC cannot be privatized. The definition of community interest that applies is also wider than the public interest test for a charity, making it more flexible.

Both the foundation trust and the community interest company are essentially reactions, the first to a perceived dead-hand model of state control, the second to the pressure of limited liability to prioritize the return of profits to investors rather than reinvestment in the business. Of course, it should be possible to deliver a CIC-style strategy through a limited liability model, without the need for a new vehicle. It is testament to how difficult this feels that such a move has proved necessary, Lazonick's cultural shift from 'retain and reinvest' to 'downsize and distribute' having become such a dominant narrative. The situation in the US reinforces this pattern. The newly created 'B-corp' device has created the legal entity of the Benefit Corporation in over twenty states, with more to come. This entity is formally allowed to consider society and the environment as well as the profit motive in their decision-making. Unfortunately, creating this separate legal construct simply reinforces the narrowness of the limited liability model by effectively endorsing its obsession with the shareholder to the exclusion of anything else. What these innovations suggest, however, is that there is scope for further policy 'nudges' in these public/private, for profit/not-for-profit hybrid models, as well as through the promotion of mutuals, co-operatives and employee ownership, given their comparative under-representation in the modern economic mix.

While it would be tempting to suggest a radical rethinking of the limited liability model, the toxicity behind the limited company is more to do with its dominance and the subsequent distortion of the marketplace, rather than about the morality of seeking profits as an end in itself. The more pragmatic policy approach would be to improve the diversity of business models through tax and regulatory changes, as Hutton's Commission suggests, to wean people off an over-reliance on the limited liability format. Current investment practice and law seem to favour a rather cynical use of the format to take profits, and if future entrepreneurs want more than this, they will need to use an alternative legal device for their organization.

Conclusion

The market will continue to change, but this book has shown how reluctant the theorists have been to update their thinking as it does so, even to accommodate the transformation of the market since Adam Smith's day. The DNA of modern capitalism is still widely believed to require an absolute commitment to competition as the primary strategy. This pre-condition is supported by the view that the individually competitive and self-interested actions of market participants are guided by an 'invisible hand' to maximize 'utility' for society as a whole. This same precondition allows supply and demand to meet at an equilibrium point, which establishes the right price. As regards individual organizations within the market, the orthodoxy of agency theory suggests that the interests of owners and employees naturally diverge, and need strenuously to be brought back into alignment. Because the shareholder is the owner of the business, corporate strategy is about maximizing their return, with the prevailing limited liability model shielding them from any downside to encourage investment. But, as we have discovered, these foundations are not as secure as they are widely presumed to be.

First, on re-examining competition, the cornerstone of capitalism, it became apparent that there is a strong mathematical case in favour of co-operation as the more usual strategy, given the rarity of zero-sum games in business. Further, while male physiology supports a tendency to compete, particularly when under pressure, this may be compounding a tendency towards sub-optimal outcomes, and ignores the role that female physiology may have to play.

Second, we have seen that the rather crucial 'invisible hand' is more the stuff of fairy tales than reality, offering a reassuring but inaccurate justification for self-interested behaviour. While order may arise out of chaos, there is no evidence that this tends towards the good, and certainly none sufficient to justify a wholesale reliance on it by the State. Indeed, laissez-faire can only skew the market in favour of those most able to participate in it, which maximizes the utility of the rich but not necessarily that of society or the world at large.

Third, the idea that utility is the best way to measure both the effectiveness and morality of the market can be justified only if the 'invisible hand' really exists. If there is no guarantee that individual utility-maximizing behaviours produce a good outcome overall, a system based on utility cannot be effortlessly moral. Similarly, we know that the idea of 'Economic Man' as a rational agent bent on maximizing utility is wildly optimistic, and just leads to confusion about the way the market actually works.

Fourth, Smith's original observation about the divergent interests of the owners and managers of joint stock companies, now widely known as agency theory, is an assumption that has cascaded a series of unfortunate outcomes. Its negative reading of psychology has led to unhelpful HR policy in general, and the disastrous ubiquity of executive shareholding in particular. This, coupled with the associated assumption of the supremacy of the shareholder, has rendered corporate strategy pathologically short-term and manipulative.

Fifth, the assumption that the price mechanism, unhindered, will settle at a scientific equilibrium, ignores the relationship between these variables and the potential for their manipulation. As well as ignoring the historical debate about 'just' prices and the 'price' of money, market pricing ignores the debate about costs and externalities. But this is a debate we can no longer afford to ignore, given the increasing risk of global 'tragedies of the commons'.

Sixth, the belief in the absolute supremacy of the shareholder, which serves as a ratchet on the assumption of agency theory, is as whimsical and wrong as the idea of the 'invisible hand'. Even ignoring the extremely limited legal case for ownership, modern patterns of shareholding make this concept rather a nonsense. Rhetorical appeals to this Santa Claus figure drive increasing short-termism, and divert the debate from wider issues of accountability. This assumption has also fuelled the exponential rise of boardroom pay, and encouraged a dangerously narrow measure of corporate performance.

Seventh, the monopolization of the limited liability model is risky in a global economy whose resilience as a system will always depend on diversity. It also exacerbates the increasingly irresponsible shareholder culture, where there is no downside. More encouragement in law and public policy of alternative models for enterprise would spread systemic risk, and create a healthier range of models for accountability and success.

These core assumptions - capitalism's 7 deadly sins - need robust challenge. While in each instance there are already moves afoot - on the fringes at least - to develop healthier models, these efforts are slow to reach the mainstream. To speed up this process, a number of specific policy changes or nudges have been mentioned in the discussion of each toxic assumption. Some of the most promising require proactivity from the state, as well as brave role-modelling by industry leaders. The most complex area to unpick is regulation about competition, and the ingrained behaviour this has created. I have rather optimistically encouraged simple transparency, and a close relationship with the regulator. Encouraging more women to hold senior positions would also adjust this culture over time. But in the short term, as Unilever discovered to their cost, companies are likely to be penalized for co-operative behaviour. So industry-wide agencies will have to take the lead on establishing safe ground for experimentation, to show the regulator that co-operation does not always descend into collusion in the hope that a more favourable regulatory climate will evolve. But many of these toxic assumptions will naturally evaporate once they have been exposed. In most cases, there are alternatives readily available, and organizations that have already blazed a trail to demonstrate that it can be done. A quiet revolution is in the gift of many business leaders, if they just shift their attention slightly and put more energy behind existing directions of travel. So what would organizations at the forefront of this revolution look like? First, they are most likely to be a small or medium-sized enterprise, because these comprise 99.9 per cent of the total number of businesses in the UK, providing 59.1 per cent of all private sector jobs. They are also a great place to start a revolution, because they are often free to experiment, under the radar. Perhaps our pioneering company started as a limited company, or its set-up was financed through bonds or loans, but it has now become employee-owned. It is still technically a company with limited liability, but its ownership status protects it from slipping into the traditional bad habits that this format can encourage.

The company is led by a female chief executive, who works with a main board and a stakeholder board to govern the enterprise as a whole. The stakeholder board meets just before the main board but discusses the same agenda, acting as an advisor to it. It comprises staff representatives of differing levels of seniority, some of whom serve a set term, and some of whom observe in rotation. It includes representatives from the unions, the customer council and the trade association, and can invite interested parties for particular meetings depending on the agenda under discussion. The community can also nominate a member, as can the group of charities that work alongside the company on the ground. It is chaired in rotation, and can require any member of the board proper to attend as it sees fit. The main board meeting is broadcast live on the company's intranet, and staff are encouraged to offer feedback both during and after the meeting. Occasionally, matters of a confidential nature need to be discussed, perhaps concerning a delicate staff or legal matter. These items are taken offline at the end of the meeting, but designated staff representatives are invited to observe these closed sessions and can challenge them if they feel that the board is being unnecessarily covert.

The members of both boards each have an upward mentor who is relatively new to the organization, and the boards use an organizational 'dashboard' to compare company performance between meetings. This is similar to a traditional scorecard, including data on finances, customers, processes and people. The customer data includes consumer feedback and brand strength, and the people data includes 'live' staff satisfaction ratings. The dashboard also includes wider measures about the health of the supply chain, and about stakeholders, competitors and known externalities as part of the company's commitment to 'full-cost' accounting.

The chief executive is currently hosting and chairing the forum, a group of competitors who meet quarterly. The chair rotates every year. The regulator attends the meetings, as from time to time do other stakeholders. Joint initiatives are reported in each company's annual report and on their websites, and the forum has strong links with similar bodies in other industries to share ideas and best practices. Currently, the forum is investigating a customer 'pay what you like' policy on parts of the offer that have long since paid back the R&D invested in them, an idea borrowed from the pharmaceutical and music industries. The company and some of its peers are also experimenting with transparent pricing, an idea borrowed from the charity sector, where customers are shown a price breakdown and the percentage of the profit element that is payable is scaled according to customer loyalty. Their other joint project is about customer access, and how they could collectively develop new business models to help the disadvantaged benefit from what the industry has to offer, either through differential pricing, charity partnerships or no-frills re-engineering.

The deputy chief executive is elected from the main board by a staff vote to serve for a three-year term, as part of a wider succession process. At the moment, the deputy is the HR director. The company has been reviewing its people strategy, and has introduced a new sifting and simulation-based selection process for all job vacancies, designed to improve diversity at all levels of the organization. Board appointments have for some time had to include on the short list a 50 per cent quota of candidates who fall into the 'diversity' category. For a while this felt tokenistic, but at least it improved the quality of the selection process and did lead to some unorthodox hires. An important part of this process was the inclusion on the selection panel of a relevant stakeholder, be they a customer, partner or junior member of staff. Now there is a good pipeline of diverse candidates for senior jobs, both internally and externally, so there are plenty of role models to help those lower down the organization see their way ahead. Flexible working has been crucial to the success of these policies, with various 'nudges' introduced around cafeteria-style benefits, flexible working, discretionary time, career breaks, percentage contracts, job-share, on-site childcare support and the option to influence the frequency of the payroll (weekly, fortnightly or monthly). No one has to work shifts, as the company has partnerships across the other two global time-zone hubs to allow those operations that require it to continue round the clock. Staff are actively involved in various local, national and international charities, and the company matches their payroll giving, supplemented by a time allocation for volunteering and annual company-wide charity initiatives.

Everyone's remuneration data is available to view on the intranet and, as co-owners, staff decide their own salaries, as well as how their package should be structured to take account of the range of benefits they choose. The only guidance offered is an annual company-wide agreement of salary bands, in order to protect the ratio between junior and senior pay, in the context of the wider discussion about how profits should be apportioned. Performance management is peer-led, and staff are assigned to an inter-departmental action-learning group that meets monthly to discuss work issues. Staff are expected to job-shadow each other to learn about the business as a whole; there is a peer-led training curriculum; and a system of secondments into customer, partner and even competitor organizations. Staff choose their own mentor and produce their own appraisals, which are updated on a rolling basis for quarterly discussion with their line manager. Some of these practices are quite a challenge for staff new to the company, who are given a personalized induction programme to help them learn how best to flourish in an employee-owned environment. At the end of their probation, there is a two-way process of dialogue about career planning and cultural fit, at which point they leave or join the company as a full shareholder.

The company does produce a traditional annual report, but this is updated throughout the year so that it is always a live document. Some of it has to be protected so that it meets official reporting requirements, but it is linked to the intranet wiki where staff also submit updates, meaning that there is a wider and more variegated report available any time an employee wants to check up on company performance. Controversially, it includes ten-year projections, which some regard as a waste of time because the future is so uncertain, while others welcome the attempt to take a longer view. It includes commentary from the wider stakeholder community too, some of which in the past has been quite critical about how long the company has taken to change its operating culture. In the financials, a range of standard ratios and metrics are used (although ROA is preferred to ROE), which feed into the board scorecard that is updated for each monthly round of board meetings. Teams are encouraged to take responsibility for their own budgets and accounting, and can select and report on their own metrics, which feed into individual appraisals and agreements about salary increases. Conventionally, these metrics include 360° staff and stakeholder feedback on behaviours as well as outcomes, mapped to the list of 'company virtues' as part of a long-standing internal tradition.

At lunchtimes, staff are encouraged to attend a variety of clubs and societies, to take a break from work and to network across the whole organization. These include the standard array of sports, crafts and hobbies, as well as some more unusual ones. One of the most popular is the investments club, where staff meet to research companies, monitor their portfolios and decide on shareholder activity. A recent triumph was engagement with one company that resulted in their board agreeing to review pricing and access, and to partner with a charity to distribute their products to developing communities in Africa under licence at a vastly reduced rate. The company is an active member of an industry-wide credit union, and many staff are involved with peer lending. Lunchtime is also a popular time for peer coaching, and a good number of employees also provide mentoring in the community to those who struggle to find jobs or manage their money. One of the other clubs is the sustainability steering group, which reports into the main board. Recently, the company has made great strides toward meeting its carbon-neutral target. It now gets all of its energy from its own biomass combined heat and power plant, sourcing waste for fuel locally and sharing the spare energy generated with other organizations in the area.

Trade union membership has continued to decline nationally, as more and more companies embrace workplace policies that honour employees and give them more say in how the business is run. But some staff still belong to them, and they remain an important part of the workplace dynamic. Their role is now rather different, though. They act more as a critical friend, monitoring international and industry trends to suggest fruitful new policies and initiatives, and where necessary championing individual causes. Their main focus, however, is their international role as ambassadors of good workplace practices, and many staff members volunteer abroad, advising organizations in the developing world about how best to structure their workplaces for sustainable success.

Many staff are actively engaged in local initiatives, as well as in citizenship activities more broadly. One part-time member of the finance department is an authority on accounting standards and serves on the International Accounting Standards Board (IASB), chairing their current review. In particular, the review is scrutinizing the treatment of externalities and the valuation of intangibles, as well as looking at details such as what counts as an expense, depreciation/amortization rules and pension liability accounting. The IASB has also conducted a global study into the cultural effectiveness of standards and is eagerly awaiting the findings. While global standardization has been a useful development, there remains concern that countries are more ready to 'comply' than they are to report in the spirit of the standards, so the global study has been looking at 'nudges' to improve reporting hygiene.

Maybe you have already heard of this company, or something like it, because many of these practices are already established in familiar organizations. Few of these practices require legislation, but they do require a change in mindset. The only thing holding your company back from becoming exemplary is the feeling that it is all too hard, and a worry that others will not follow suit. But perhaps you could pick just a couple of these measures to use as nudges towards something better. Where would you start?

And as a consumer, where would you start? Perhaps next time your bank statement arrives you could pause to examine it in more detail. Who do you bank with, and why? What does your statement say about how you are currently casting your own 'votes' in our global marketplace? Could you change your spending habits to more accurately reflect the kind of marketplace you want? And when reports on your pension or other investments arrive, could you read them carefully to check how others are investing on your behalf? For instance, in the UK, ShareAction has set up a website at http://greenlightcampaign.org.uk for you to contact your pension provider direct to check their mandate for managing your funds. And how involved are you in consumer action through petition sites like 38degrees.org.uk, Avaaz.org or change.org?

On 6 May 1954 at the Iffley Road Racetrack in Oxford, Norris McWhirter announced to 3,000 spectators:

> Ladies and gentlemen, here is the result of Event 9, the one mile: 1st, Number 41, R G Bannister, Amateur Athletic Association and formerly of Exeter and Merton Colleges, Oxford, with a time which is a new meeting and track record, and which - subject to ratification - will be a new English Native, British National, All-Comers, European, British Empire and World Record. The time was 3 minutes, 59.4 seconds.

After Bannister broke the record, he held it for only 46 days. He had that most important asset, a 'first follower', in the person of the Australian John Landy. It was Landy who first broke Bannister's record, showing that the feat was not just a one-off, and attracting others to try. It was broken again five times over the next decade. The current record, set in Rome in

July 1999, is held by Hicham El Guerrouj of Morocco, with a time that would once have been considered impossible: 3 minutes, 43.13 seconds.

While trailblazers are important, it is when they start attracting a following that a trend catches on. Many of the healthy practices mentioned in this book are already in use in exceptional organizations across the sectors, and across the globe. But we need some brave 'first followers' to start a trend. As we have seen, the market is infinitely susceptible to nudges. All you need to do is to start by questioning these seven assumptions every time you hear them or see them in print. That would be enough to start a revolution in thinking that could end up healing not only our broken economy but the lives of many around the world.

References and further reading

Advertising Age, 'The Advertising Century' (29 March 1999) at http://adage.com/special-reports/theadvertisingcentury/110

Akin, Çiğdem & Kose, M Ayhan, 'Changing nature of north-south linkages: stylized facts and explanations', IMF Working Paper WP/07/280 (2007) at http://www.imf.org/external/pubs/ft/wp/2007/wp07280.pdf

Allingham, Michael, *Choice Theory* (Oxford: OUP: 2002)

Ariely, Dan, *Predictably Irrational* (London: Harper Collins: 2009)

Aristotle, *Metaphysics*, Book IX Part I (translated by WD Ross) at http://classics.mit.edu//Aristotle/metaphysics.9.ix.html

— *Nicomachean Ethics*, Book II (translated by WD Ross) at http://classics.mit.edu/Aristotle/nicomachaen.2.ii.html

— *On The Soul*, Book II Part I (translated by JA Smith) at http://classics.mit.edu//Aristotle/soul.2.ii.html

— *Physics*, Book III Part I (translated by RP Hardie & RK Gaye) at http://classics.mit.edu//Aristotle/physics.3.iii.html

Associated Press, 'Sweden moving towards cashless economy' (18 March 2012) at http://www.cbsnews.com/news/sweden-moving-towards-cashless-economy/

Atherton, John & Skinner, Hannah (eds), *Through the Eye of a Needle* (Peterborough: Epworth: 2007)

Axelrod, Robert, *The Evolution of Co-operation* (London: Penguin: 1990)

Axelrod, Robert & Hamilton, William, 'The Evolution of Cooperation', *Science* 211 (1981), pp.1390-1396

Bakan, Joel, *The Corporation* (London: Constable & Robinson: 2004)

Bamford, James, 'Inside the matrix', *Wired* 20:04 (April 2012)

Bartov, Eli, Givoly, Dan & Hayn, Carla, 'The rewards for meeting or beating earnings expectations', *Journal of Accounting and Economics* 33 (2002), pp.173-204

Begley, Sharon, *The Plastic Mind* (London: Constable: 2009)

Beinhocker, Eric D, *The Origin of Wealth* (London: Random House: 2007)

Benjamin, Ludy T, Jr, *A Brief History of Modern Psychology* (Oxford: Blackwell: 2007)

Berle, Adolf A & Means, Gardiner C, *The Modern Corporation and Private Property* (New York, NY: Macmillan: 1932)

Best Companies, 'Best Companies the Workplace Engagement Specialists' (2013) at http://democracy.merthyr.gov.uk/documents/s19389/13.05.22%20-%20Item%2022%20-%20Workforce%20Engagement%20and%20Retention.pdf

Bhargava, Alok, 'An econometric analysis of dividends and share repurchases by US firms', *Journal of the Royal Statistical Society A* 173:3 (2010), pp.631-656

Biggar, Nigel, 'Saving the "secular": the public vocation of moral theology', *Journal of Religious Ethics* 37:1 (2009)

Black, Michael, *The Theology of the Corporation: Sources and History of the Corporate Relation in Christian Tradition* (PhD thesis: University of Oxford: October 2009)

Block, Fred, *Postindustrial Possibilities* (Berkeley, CA: University of California Press: 1990)

Bolchover, David, *The Living Dead* (Chichester: Capstone: 2005)

Bonhoeffer, Dietrich, *Ethics* (New York, NY: Touchstone: 1995)

Botsman, Rachel & Rogers, Roo, *What's Mine Is Yours* (London: Collins: 2011)

Brander, James A & Lewis, Tracy R, 'Oligopoly and financial structure: the limited liability effect', *The American Economic Review* 76:5 (Dec 1986), pp.956-970

Brander, James A & Spencer, Barbara J, 'Moral hazard and limited liability: implications for the theory of the firm', *International Economic Review* 30:4 (1989), pp.833-849

Brown, Lester R, *Plan B 4.0: Mobilizing to Save Civilization* (2009) at http://www.earth-policy.org/books/pb4/PB4ch10_ss2

— *World on the Edge* (London: WW Norton & Co: 2011)

Brown, Malcolm, *After the Market* (Oxford: Peter Lang: 2004)

Brownlie, Nikki, *Trade Union Membership 2011* (London: BIS: 2011) at http://www.bis.gov.uk/analysis/statistics/trade-union/union-membership-2011

Buckingham, Marcus & Coffman, Curt, *First, Break All the Rules* (New York, NY: Simon & Schuster: 1999)

Buckley, Susan L, *Teachings on Usury in Judaism, Christianity and Islam* (Lewiston, NY: Edwin Mellen Press: 2000)

Burke, Peter, Harrison, Brian & Slack, Paul (eds), *Civil Histories* (Oxford: OUP: 2000)

Campbell, Andrew, Finkelstein, Sydney & Whitehead, Jo, *Think Again* (Harvard, MA: Harvard Business School Press: 2009)

Chang, Ha-Joon, *23 Things They Don't Tell You About Capitalism* (London: Allen Lane: 2010)

Chen, Stephen, 'CEOs and Financial Misreporting' in Millar, Carla & Poole, Eve (eds): *Ethical Leadership* (Basingstoke: Palgrave: 2010)

Cheng, Jonathan & Strasburg, Jenny, 'Trading Volumes Sink Even as Stocks Rally', *Wall Street Journal* (4 October 2010)

Christian Aid, 'Master or servant' (2001) at http://www.christianaid.org.uk/Images/master_or_servant.pdf

Coates, John M, Gurnell, Mark & Sarnyai, Zoltan, 'From molecule to market: steroid hormones and financial risk-taking', *Philosophical Transactions of the Royal Society B* 365 (2010), pp.331–343

Collins, Jim & Porras, Jerry, *Built to Last* (London: Random House: 2004)

Cooper, Michael J, Gulen, Huseyin, & Rau, P Raghavendra, 'Performance for pay? The relation between CEO incentive compensation and future stock price performance' (30 January 2013) at http://papers.ssrn.com/sol3/papers.cfm?abstract_id=1572085

Cram, Tony, *Smarter Pricing* (London: FT Prentice Hall: 2005)

Davies, E Mervyn, 'Women on boards' (February 2010) at http://www.bis.gov.uk/news/topstories/2011/Feb/women-on-boards#women

de Soto, Hernando, *The Mystery of Capital* (London: Black Swan: 2001)

Decety, J, Jackson, PL, & Sommerville, JA, 'The neural bases of cooperation and competition: an fMRI investigation', *NeuroImage* 23 (2004), pp.744–751

Doctrine Commission of the Church of England, *Being Human* (Church House Publishing: 2003)

Doidge, Norman, *The Brain That Changes Itself* (London: Penguin: 2008)

Dow, Sheila, 'Enlightening economics', *RSA Journal* (Winter 2010), pp.24–27

Dransfield, Sarah, 'A tale of two Britains', *Oxfam Policy Paper* (17 March 2014) at http://policy-practice.oxfam.org.uk/publications/a-tale-of-two-britains-inequality-in-the-uk-314152

Dutton, Kevin, *Flipnosis* (London: Arrow: 2010)

Ellis, Markman, *The Coffee-House: A Cultural History* (London: Phoenix: 2004)

Erdal, David, *Local Heroes* (London: Viking: 2008)

Fama, Eugene F & Jensen, Michael C, 'Separation of ownership and control', *Journal of Law and Economics* 26:2 (1983), pp.301–325

— 'Agency problems and residual claims', *Journal of Law and Economics* 26:2 (1983), pp.327–349

Faure-Grimaud, Antoine, 'Optimal debt contracts and product market competition: the limited liability effect revisited', *European Economic Review* 44:10 (2000)

Ferguson, Niall, *The Ascent of Money* (London: Allen Lane: 2008)

Fisher, Greg & Ormerod, Paul, *Beyond the PLC* (London: Civitas: 2013)

Flyvbjerg, Bent, *Making Social Science Matter* (Cambridge: CUP: 2002)

FSA. *The Turner Review: A Regulatory Response to the Global Banking Crisis* (March 2009)

Fukuyama, Francis, *Trust* (New York, NY: Free Press: 1995)

Ghoshal, Sumantra, 'Bad management theories are destroying good management practices', *Academy of Management Learning and Education* 4:1 (2005), pp.75–91

Gladwell, Malcolm, *Blink* (London: Penguin: 2006)

GMI Ratings, '2012 Preliminary CEO Pay Survey' (3 May 2012) at http://www3.gmiratings.com/wp-content/uploads/2012/05/GMI-Release-2012-0503.pdf

Gorringe, Timothy, *Capital and the Kingdom: Theological Ethics and Economic Order* (London: SPCK: 1994)

— *Fair Shares: Ethics and the Global Economy* (London: Thames & Hudson: 1999)

Grant, Adam, 'Does studying economics breed greed?', *Psychology Today* (22 October 2013) at http://www.psychologytoday.com/blog/give-and-take/201310/does-studying-economics-breed-greed

Griffin, Douglas, *The Emergence of Leadership: Linking Self-organization and Ethics* (London: Routledge: 2002)

Gueguen, Gaël, Pellegrin-Boucher, Estelle, & Torres, Olivier, 'Between cooperation and competition: the benefits of collective strategies within business ecosystems', *European Institute for Advanced Studies in Management*, 2nd Workshop on Co-opetition Strategy, Milan, Italy, September 2006

Guiso, Luigi, Sapienza, Paola & Zingales, Luigi, 'People's opium? Religion and economic attitudes', *NBER Working Paper Series* #9237 (2002)

Haldane, Andrew G, 'Control rights (and wrongs)', Wincott Annual Memorial Lecture (October 2011) at http://www.bankofengland.co.uk/publications/Documents/speeches/2011/speech525.pdf

— 'The doom loop', *London Review of Books* 34:4 (February 2012), pp.21–22

Hamel, Gary, 'Strategy as revolution', *Harvard Business Review* (July–August 1996)

Hampden-Turner, Charles & Trompenaars, Fons, *The Seven Cultures of Capitalism* (London: Piatkus: 1994)

Hardin, Garrett, 'Tragedy of the commons', *Science* 162 (1968), pp.1243–1248

Hart, Hugh, 'Crowdsourced movie studio creates a bold new kind of sci-fi series', *Wired* (15 March 2012), at http://www.wired.com/underwire/2012/03/the-new-kind-anime-series/

Harvey, David, *Seventeen Contradictions and the End of Capitalism* (London: Profile Books: 2014)

Hay, Donald A & Kreider, Alan (eds), *Christianity and the Culture of Economics* (Cardiff: University of Wales Press: 2001)

Hertz, Noreena, *The Silent Takeover* (New York, NY: Harper Business: 2003)

Howie, Michael, 'Fake goods are fine, says EU study', *Telegraph* (29 August 2010) at http://www.telegraph.co.uk/finance/newsbysector/retailandconsumer/7969335/Fake-goods-are-fine-says-EU-study.html

Hughes, John, *The End of Work: Theological Critiques of Capitalism* (Oxford: Blackwell: 2007)

Hume, David, *An Inquiry Concerning Human Understanding* Section XII, Part III (1748) at http://www.earlymoderntexts.com/pdfs/hume1748.pdf

Hutton, Will, *Them and Us* (London: Abacus: 2011)

International Forum on Globalization, *Alternatives to Economic Globalization* (San Francisco, CA: Berrett Koehler: 2002)

International Labour Organization, 'Income inequalities in the age of financial globalization', *World of Work Report* (2008)

Ireland, Paddy, 'Company law and the myth of shareholder ownership', *The Modern Law Review* 62:1 (1999), pp.32–57

Iyengar, Sheena, *The Art of Choosing* (London: Abacus: 2011)

James, Oliver, *Affluenza* (London: Vermillion: 2007)

— *The Selfish Capitalist* (London: Vermillion: 2008)

Janis, Irving L, *Victims of Groupthink* (Oxford: Houghton Mifflin: 1972)

Jenkins, David, *Market Whys and Human Wherefores* (London: Continuum: 2004)

Jensen, Michael C & Meckling, William H, 'Theory of the firm: managerial behavior, agency costs and ownership structure', *Journal of Financial Economics* 3:4 (1976), pp.305–360

Johnson, Neil, Zhao, Guannan, Hunsader, Eric, Meng, Jing, Ravindar, Amith, Carran, Spencer & Tivnan, Brian, 'Financial black swans driven by ultrafast machine ecology' available at http://arxiv.org/ftp/arxiv/papers/1202/1202.1448.pdf

Kahneman, Daniel, 'A perspective on judgment and choice: mapping bounded rationality', *American Psychologist* (2003), pp.697–720

Kandasamy, Narayanan, Hardy, Ben, Page, Lionel, Schaffner, Markus, Graggaber, Johann, Powlson, Andrew S, Fletcher, Paul C, Gurnell, Mark & Coates, John, 'Cortisol shifts financial risk preferences', *Proceedings of the National Academy of Sciences* III:9 (2014), pp.3608–3613

Kay, John, 'The Kay Review of UK equity markets and long-term decision making', (2012) available at http://www.bis.gov.uk/assets/biscore/business-law/docs/k/12-917-kay-review-of-equity-markets-final-report.pdf

Klein, Naomi, *No Logo* (London: Flamingo: 2001)

Kleiner, Art, *Who Really Matters* (New York, NY: Crown Business: 2003)

Kuo, Frances E & Sullivan, William C, 'Environment and Crime in the Inner City - Does Vegetation Reduce Crime?' *Environment and Behavior* (2001) 33:343 at http://nfs.unl.edu/documents/communityforestry/KuoSullivanenvironmentandcrime.pdf

Langholm, Odd, *The Legacy of Scholasticism in Economic Thought* (Cambridge: CUP: 1998)

Lawson, Tony, 'Mathematical modelling and ideology in the economics academy', available at http://discussion.world-economicsassociation.org/?post=mathematical-modelling-and-ideology-in-the-economics-academy-competing-explanations-of- the-failings-of-the-modern-discipline

Lazonick, William & O'Sullivan, Mary, 'Maximising shareholder value: a new ideology for corporate governance', *Economy and Society* 29:1 (February 2000), pp.13–35

— 'Everyone is paying price for share buy-backs', *Financial Times* (25 September 2008)

— 'The explosion of executive pay and the erosion of American prosperity', *Industry Studies Association* Annual Conference (May 2010), at http://www.theairnet.org/files/research/lazonick/Lazonick%20Explosion%20and%20Erosion%20ISA%20revised%2020100922.pdf

Lewis, Michael, *Flash Boys* (London: Allen Lane: 2014)

Lobban, Michael, 'Corporate identity and limited liability in France and England 1825–67', *Anglo-American Law Review* (1996), pp.397–440

Logsdon, Jeanne M & Van Buren, Harry J, III, 'Beyond the proxy vote: dialogues between shareholder activists and corporations', *Journal of Business Ethics* 87 (2009), pp.353–365

Lucking-Reiley, David, Bryan, Doug, Prasad, Naghi, & Reeves, Daniel, 'Pennies from eBay: the determinants of price in online auctions', *Vanderbilt University Working Paper* 00-W03 (2000), at http://www.vanderbilt.edu/econ/wparchive/workpaper/vu00-w03.pdf

MacIntyre, Alasdair, *After Virtue* (London: Duckworth: 2003)

MacLeod, David & Clarke, Nita, 'Engaging for success: enhancing performance through employee engagement', Department for Business, Innovation and Skills (2009), at http://dera.ioe.ac.uk/1810/1/file52215.pdf

Manner, Mikko, 'CEOs and Corporate Social Performance' in Millar, Carla & Poole, Eve (eds): *Ethical Leadership* (Basingstoke: Palgrave: 2010)

Martin, Roger L, *Fixing the Game* (Boston, MA: HBRP: 2011)

McKinsey & Company, 'Women at the top of corporations: making it happen', *Women Matter* 4 (2010), at http://www.mckinsey.com/locations/swiss/news_publications/pdf/women_matter_2010_4.pdf

Melitz, Jacques & Winch, Donald (eds), *Religious Thought and Economic Society: Four Chapters of an Unfinished Work by Jacob Viner* (Durham, NC: Duke University Press: 1978)

Micklethwait, John & Wooldridge, Adrian, *The Company* (London: Phoenix: 2003)

Midgley, Mary, *Wickedness* (London: Routledge: 1997)

— *The Solitary Self* (Durham: Acumen: 2010)

Milbank, John, 'Stale expressions: the management-shaped church', *Studies in Christian Ethics* 21:1 (April 2008), pp.117–128

Muller, Jerry Z, *The Mind and the Market* (New York, NY: Anchor Books: 2002)

Murphy, Richard, *The Courageous State* (London: Searching Finance: 2011)

Nalebuff, Barry J & Brandenburger, Adam M, *Co-opetition* (London: HarperCollinsBusiness: 1996)

Nash, John F, Jr, *Essays on Game Theory* (Cheltenham: Edward Elgar: 1996)

Neuwirth, Robert, *Stealth of Nations* (New York, NY: Pantheon Books: 2011)

New Economics Foundation, 'Buying local worth 400 per cent more' (7 March 2005) at http://www.neweconomics.org/press/entry/buying-local-worth-400-per-cent-more

North, Douglass C, *Institutions, Institutional Change and Economic Performance* (Cambridge: CUP: 1990)

Nowak, Martin with Highfield, Roger, *Super Cooperators* (Edinburgh: Canongate: 2011)

O'Connell, Dominic, 'Revealed: which bosses deserve their bonuses', *The Sunday Times* (19 February 2012)

Office for National Statistics, *Share Ownership Survey 2010* (Newport: ONS: 2012), at http://www.ons.gov.uk/ons/dcp171778_257476.pdf

On Device Research, 'Popularity of mobile finance in emerging markets presents new m-commerce opportunities' (9 May 2012) at https://ondeviceresearch.com/blog/mobile-finance-in-emerging-markets-mcommerce-opportunities

Ormerod, Paul, *Butterfly Economics* (London: Faber & Faber: 1999)

— *Why Most Things Fail* (London: Faber & Faber: 2005)

Ownership Commission, *Plurality, Stewardship & Engagement* (Borehamwood: Mutuo: 2012)

Parker, Martin, *Against Management* (Cambridge: Polity: 2002)

Pattison, Stephen, *The Faith of the Managers: When Management Becomes Religion* (London: Cassell: 1997)

Piketty, Thomas, *Capital in the Twenty-First Century* (Cambridge, MA: Harvard University Press: 2014)

Plant, Raymond, *Politics, Theology and History* (Cambridge: CUP: 2001)

Polanyi, Karl, *The Great Transformation* (Boston, MA: Beacon Press: 2001)

Poole, Eve, 'On the use of language in the anti-capitalist debate', *European Journal of Business Ethics* 59:4 (July 2005), pp.319-325

— 'Baptizing management', *Studies in Christian Ethics* 21:1 (2008), pp.85-97

Prahalad, CK, *The Fortune at the Bottom of the Pyramid* (Upper Saddle River, NJ: Wharton School Publishing: 2006)

Reder, Melvin W, 'Chicago economics: permanence and change', *Journal of Economic Literature* 20 (1982), pp.1-38

Ridley, Matt, *The Origins of Virtue* (London: Penguin: 1996)

Sachs, Jeffrey, *Common Wealth: Economics for a Crowded Planet* (London: Penguin: 2008)

Salmon, Felix, 'Recipe for disaster: the formula that killed Wall Street', *Wired* 17:03 (February 2009)
— 'Why going public sucks', *Wired* 20:04 (April 2012)
Samuels, Warren J, with Johnson, MF & Perry, WH, *Erasing the Invisible Hand* (Cambridge: CUP: 2011)
Sandel, Michael, *BBC Reith Lecture* (June 2009) at http://www.bbc.co.uk/programmes/b00kt7rg
Schwartz, Tony, 'People leave managers, not jobs', *Fast Company* Issue 40 (January 2000), p. 398
Sedgwick, Peter, *The Market Economy and Christian Ethics* (Cambridge: CUP: 1999)
Semler, Ricardo, *Maverick!* (London: Random House: 2001)
Shaw, Graham, *God in Our Hands* (London: SCM Press: 1987)
Skinner, Quentin & Price, Russell (eds), *Machiavelli's The Prince* (Cambridge: CUP: 1991)
Smith, Adam, *The Wealth of Nations Books I–III* (London: Penguin: 1997)
— *The Wealth of Nations Books IV–V* (London: Penguin: 1999)
— *The Theory of Moral Sentiments* (Cambridge: CUP: 2002)
Solomon, Robert C, 'Victims of circumstances? A defense of virtue ethics in business', *Business Ethics Quarterly* 13:1 (Jan 2003), pp.43–62
Stern, Stefan, 'How to live long and prosper', *Financial Times*, (12 March 2012), at http://www.ft.com/cms/s/0/02682732-6855-11e1-a6cc-00144feabdc0.html#ixzz1p0uJ0000
Stichter, Matt, 'Virtues, skills, and right action', *Ethical Theory and Moral Practice* 14:1 (2011), pp.73–86
Stiglitz, Joseph E, *Globalization and Its Discontents* (London: Penguin: 2002)
— 'Wall Street's toxic message', *Vanity Fair* (July 2009)
Stoner, James AF & Wankel, Charles (eds), *Innovative Approaches to Reducing Global Poverty* (Charlotte, NC: Information Age: 2007)
Surowiecki, James, *The Wisdom of Crowds* (London: Abacus: 2005)
Tawney, RH, *Religion and the Rise of Capitalism* (London: Pelican Books: 1948)

Taylor, Shelley E, Klein, Laura Cousino, Lewis, Brian P, Gruenewald, Tara L, Gurung, Regan AR & Updegraff, John A, 'Biobehavioral responses to stress in females: tend-and-befriend, not fight-or-flight', *Psychological Review* 107:3 (2000), pp.411–429

Thaler, Richard H & Sunstein, Cass R, *Nudge* (New Haven, CT: Yale University Press: 2008)

UN Global Compact, 'A new agenda for the board of directors', (January 2012), at http://www.unglobalcompact.org/docs/news_events/9.1_news_archives/2012_01_27/Lead-board-loresR.pdf

Watzlawick, Paul, Weakland, John & Fisch, Richard, *Change* (New York, NY: WW Norton & Co: 1974)

Weber, Max, *The Protestant Ethic and the Spirit of Capitalism* (London: Routledge: 2002)

Wilkinson, Richard & Pickett, Kate, *The Spirit Level* (London: Penguin: 2010)

Wille, Edgar & Barham, Kevin, *A Role for Business at the Bottom of the Pyramid* (Ashridge: Ashridge Business School: 2009)

Williams, Rowan, 'From Faust to Frankenstein', *Prospect* 194 (May 2012), pp.26–30

Wiseman, Richard, *59 Seconds* (Basingstoke: Pan Macmillan: 2010)

Yong, Ed, 'How the science of swarms can help us fight cancer and predict the future', *Wired* (March 2013), at http://www.wired.com/wiredscience/2013/03/powers-of-swarms/

Zoellner, Tom, *The Heartless Stone* (New York, NY: St Martin's Press: 2006)

Index